# Contents

W9-CBE-301

# A Good Pet

My sister has a new pet. Can you guess what it is? It is not a dog, a cat, or a bird. It is a pet she can ride. It's a pony!

The pony has a white star on her nose. My sister gave her the name Star. Star is a cute pony. Although she is full-grown, she is little. Sometimes I help my sister feed and brush Star. We keep her stall clean, too. Sometimes my sister lets me ride her pony. When I brought an apple for Star, she came to me. Star is a good pet. I hope that someday I will have a pony of my own.

**Find It!**
Read the spelling words.
Check off the words you can find in the story.

- ☑ came
- ☑ name
- ☑ ride
- ☐ bone
- ☑ cute
- ☐ mine
- ☑ dog
- ☑ cat
- ☑ bird
- ☑ pet

How many spelling words did you find? _____

# Spelling Practice

| Read and Spell | Copy and Spell | Spell It Again! |
|---|---|---|
| 1. came | _____ | _____ |
| 2. name | _____ | _____ |
| 3. ride | _____ | _____ |
| 4. bone | _____ | _____ |
| 5. cute | _____ | _____ |
| 6. mine | _____ | _____ |
| 7. dog | _____ | _____ |
| 8. cat | _____ | _____ |
| 9. bird | _____ | _____ |
| 10. pet | _____ | _____ |

# Word Meanings

Skills:

Using Context Clues to Identify Missing Words

Writing Complete Sentences

Write the missing words to finish the sentences.

1. That _____ little turtle is _____.

    bone          mine          cute

2. A singing _____ makes a good _____.

    pet          ride          bird

3. What will you _____ your new _____?

    name          cat          came

4. My _____ chews a _____.

    bone          cute          dog

5. My dad _____ to see me _____ the pony.

    name          came          ride

Write a sentence using the words **mine** and **cute**.

_____

_____

Write a sentence using the words **bird** and **name**.

_____

_____

# Word Study

Fill in the missing vowels to make spelling words.

| came | name | ride | bone | cute |
|------|------|------|------|------|
| mine | dog | cat | bird | pet |

d ___ g

c ____ m ____

m ___ n ___

b ____ rd

c ___ t

c ___ t ___

n ___ m ___

b ___ n ___

r ___ d ___

p ___ t

Circle each spelling word.

petcatminebonenamebirddogcuteridecame

cameridecutedogbirdnamebon6minecatpet

minedogcutecatbonebirdridepetnamecame

# Reading Sentences

> A sentence is a complete thought.
> Every sentence has two parts.
> - It names something or someone.
> - It tells what that something or someone is or does.
>
> Claire feeds her dog every day.
>
> Bib wags his tail.

Circle the complete sentences. Draw a line through the groups of words that are <u>not</u> sentences.

1. Over the fence.

2. The dog jumps for the ball.

3. Jake took his puppy for a ride.

4. In the wagon.

5. A nice pet.

6. The cute puppy was happy.

7. My dog likes to sit in the wagon.

8. Tana's kitten is soft and sweet.

# Pet Names

The names of people, pets, and specific places and things begin with capital letters.

> Tracy's rabbit is fast.
> He came from Sunrise Farm.
> Brownie likes the garden.

Circle the names that need capital letters. Then write them on the lines.

1. tina and gabe are lucky.

   _____

2. Their dad took them to white city.

   _____

3. They went to sunrise animal home.

   _____

4. mr. chang takes care of lost animals.

   _____

5. There was a mother cat named missy.

   _____

6. missy had six cute kittens.

   _____

7. One of missy's kittens was named strawberry.

   _____

8. gabe got a kitten named jam.

   _____

# Capital I

▶ Use a capital letter for the word that names yourself—I.

**I wish I had a hamster.**

Circle the sentences that have a capital **I**.
Fix the sentences that should have a capital **I**.

1. I have a new dog.

   _____

2. Can i train him to do tricks?

   _____

3. I hope so.

   _____

4. Mom and i will teach him to speak.

   _____

5. i tell him to speak.

   _____

6. when he barks, i give him a treat.

   _____

7. I hug him and pat him.

   _____

8. i have fun, and so does my dog.

   _____

# Pet Questions

Ask three people about pets. Write their answers below. Use capital letters for names of people and pets.

Ask these questions:
- What kind of pet do you like?
- What pet name do you like?

Example: Jose likes dogs.
Jose likes the pet name Socks.

1. _____ likes _____.
   (name)                      (kind of pet)

   _____ likes the pet name _____.
   (name)                                      (pet name)

2. _____ likes _____.
   (name)                      (kind of pet)

   _____ likes the pet name _____.
   (name)                                      (pet name)

3. _____ likes _____.
   (name)                      (kind of pet)

   _____ likes the pet name _____.
   (name)                                      (pet name)

# Lost and Found

Pretend you lost a pet. Make a sign to put up in your neighborhood. Tell about the pet. Draw a picture of your lost pet.

| came | name | ride | bone | cute |
| mine | dog | cat | bird | pet |

## ✓ Check Your Story

○ I used a capital letter for names.

○ I checked my spelling.

 **TEST YOUR SKILLS**

# A Good Pet

## My Spelling Test

Find the correct answer. Fill in the circle.

1. Which group of words is a complete sentence?
   - ○ A cute dog.
   - ○ Your new kitten.
   - ○ We found a lost dog.

2. Which sentence has the correct capital letters?
   - ○ My horse daisy is a good jumper.
   - ○ Travis trained his dog Tucker to roll over.
   - ○ I like your pet skunk twinkle.

3. Which sentence has the correct capital letter?
   - ○ You and i like cats.
   - ○ Mom said I may feed the fish.
   - ○ May i walk the dog?

4. Which sentence needs a capital letter?
   - ○ The brown and white dog is mine.
   - ○ I think rex wants a bone.
   - ○ Here is a bone for your dog.

Ask someone to test you on the spelling words.

1. _____

2. _____

3. _____

4. _____

5. _____

6. _____

7. _____

8. _____

9. _____

10. _____

5. Write the sentence correctly.

### i think we should nam that kute berd princess

_____

_____

Spell & Write • EMC 4538 • © Evan-Moor Corp.

# Busy Bees

Did you know that bees have special jobs? The queen bee only has one job. She lays eggs. But worker bees do different jobs as they grow. A worker bee's first job is to clean the hive. When a worker bee is three days old, its body makes food. It feeds the unborn baby bees. Many days later, the worker bee begins to make wax. The wax is used to build new honeycomb cells.

Next, the bee becomes a guard. Guards watch over the hive. They sting bears or people who try to get the hive's honey. When it is three weeks old, the bee must fly away from the hive. All alone, it looks for food in fields and flowers. Worker bees have a busy life!

## Find It!

Read the spelling words.
Check off the words you can find in the story.

| | | | | |
|---|---|---|---|---|
| ☑ she | ☑ he | ☑ got | ☑ see | ☑ bee |
| ☑ queen | ☑ hive | ☑ sting | ☑ fly | ☑ buzz |

How many spelling words did you find? _____

# Spelling Practice

| Read and Spell | Copy and Spell | Spell It Again! |
| --- | --- | --- |
| 1. she | _____ | _____ |
| 2. he | _____ | _____ |
| 3. got | _____ | _____ |
| 4. see | _____ | _____ |
| 5. bee | _____ | _____ |
| 6. queen | _____ | _____ |
| 7. hive | _____ | _____ |
| 8. sting | _____ | _____ |
| 9. fly | _____ | _____ |
| 10. buzz | _____ | _____ |

# What's Missing?

Finish the spelling words in each sentence.

| | | | | |
|---|---|---|---|---|
| she | he | got | see | bee |
| queen | hive | sting | fly | buzz |

1. Did you s_____ something f_____ by?

2. S_____ heard something b_____.

3. H_____ has a h_____ at the bee farm.

4. The q_____ b_____ lives in there.

5. We g_____ some honey from the farm.

6. A fly won't s_____ you.

Finish the spelling words to complete the crossword puzzles.

# Spell and Write

Circle the misspelled words. Write them correctly on the lines.

1. I sea Grandma holding a pie.  _____

2. Shee put the pie in the window.  _____

3. I saw a bee flie by the pie.  _____

4. The bee went buzzz.  _____

5. The dog gott the bee.  _____

6. And hee also got the pie.  _____

Unscramble the spelling words and write them correctly.

| ebe | qeenu |
|-----|-------|
| _____ | _____ |
| evih | tgins |
| _____ | _____ |

# Parts of a Sentence

A sentence is a complete thought.
Every sentence has two parts.

- It names something or someone.
- It tells what that something or someone is or does.

**Jim looks for butterflies.**

Circle the part of the sentence that names something or someone. Underline the part of the sentence that tells what that something or someone does.

(Jessica) reads about bees.

1. The boys watched a trail of ants.

2. Carlos sees a grasshopper.

3. I see an orange butterfly.

4. Marty likes to look at spider webs.

5. Mrs. Rose teaches us about bees.

6. Dena stayed away from the hive.

7. Emma and Jade hear crickets.

8. Grandfather got ladybugs for the garden.

# All About Nouns

A noun is a word that names a person, place, or thing.

Kate is at the park with her book about bugs.
(person)    (place)    (thing)    (thing)

Write each noun under the correct heading.

| garden | hive | boy | fly | forest |
| queen | teacher | pond | bee | |

| Person | Place | Thing |
|--------|-------|-------|
| _____ | _____ | _____ |
| _____ | _____ | _____ |
| _____ | _____ | _____ |

Use nouns from above to finish the sentences.

1. The _____ saw a _____

   in the _____.

2. Can the _____ find the _____?

# All About Verbs

> Verbs are words that tell what is happening or has already happened. They name an action.
>
> Bees fly to the hive. (what is happening)
> The bees made honey. (what has already happened)

Read the sentences. Circle the verbs.

1. We (see) the hive in a tree.

2. We fly to the hive.

3. The queen bee laid her eggs.

4. We worked all day.

5. We feed the baby bees in the hive.

6. A hungry bear smells our honey.

7. We buzz around the hive.

8. We sting the bear.

9. He stays away from our hive.

10. We fly to lots of flowers.

# A New Bug

You just discovered a new kind of bug! Answer the questions about your bug. Then draw a picture of your bug on the leaf.

1. What is your bug's name?

_____

2. What size and shape is your bug?

_____

3. What color is your bug?

_____

4. Where does your bug live?

_____

5. How does your bug get around?

_____

6. What is special about your bug?

_____

# Me, the Bee

You woke up this morning to find that you are a worker bee.
How does it feel to be so small? What do you do all day?
Tell your story. Use as many spelling words as you can.

| | | | | |
|---|---|---|---|---|
| she | he | got | see | bee |
| queen | hive | sting | fly | buzz |

_____

_____

_____

_____

_____

_____

_____

_____

_____

_____

✔ **Check Your Story**

○ I wrote complete sentences.
○ I checked my spelling.

## Busy Bees

## My Spelling Test

Find the correct answer. Fill in the circle.

1. Read this sentence:
   The boys read a butterfly book.
   Which part names someone?
   ○ The boys
   ○ read a butterfly book.

2. Read this sentence:
   My friend Parker likes ladybugs.
   Which part tells what someone does?
   ○ My friend Parker
   ○ likes ladybugs.

3. Which word is a noun?
   ○ see
   ○ got
   ○ bee

4. Which word is a verb?
   ○ work
   ○ hive
   ○ queen

Ask someone to test you on the spelling words.

1. _____

2. _____

3. _____

4. _____

5. _____

6. _____

7. _____

8. _____

9. _____

10. _____

5. Write the sentence correctly.

   **hee can hear a bea bozz near the hiv**

   _____

   _____

Spell & Write • EMC 4538 • © Evan-Moor Corp.

# At the Gym

On Saturday, I go to the gym. My friend Amy and I both go there. Last week, we had fun in class. We started with warm-ups. Then we got into teams. Our team wanted to win. We lined up. I put a beanbag on my head. I had to walk from one end of the gym to the other. I got a score of two points. Amy was the next one in line. She put the beanbag on her head. She walked from one end to the other. Our team was fast, but we didn't win this time.

Next, we learned how to make a bridge. You must bend your back and look at the sky. We did log rolls, too. Just hold your arms together over your head. Hold your legs together. Then roll across the mat. Amy and I will practice at home.

**Find It!**

Read the spelling words.
Check off the words you can find in the story.

| ✓ send | ✓ end | ✓ both | ✓ fast | ✓ last |
|--------|-------|--------|--------|--------|
| ✓ must | ✓ just | ✓ team | ✓ win | ✓ score |

How many spelling words did you find? _____

# Spelling Practice

| Read and Spell | Copy and Spell | Spell It Again! |
|---|---|---|
| 1. send | _____ | _____ |
| 2. end | _____ | _____ |
| 3. both | _____ | _____ |
| 4. fast | _____ | _____ |
| 5. last | _____ | _____ |
| 6. must | _____ | _____ |
| 7. just | _____ | _____ |
| 8. team | _____ | _____ |
| 9. win | _____ | _____ |
| 10. score | _____ | _____ |

# Puzzle Time

Fill in the boxes with the spelling words.

| send | end | both | fast | last |
| must | just | team | win | score |

1.

2.

3.

4.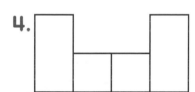

5.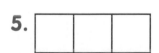

6.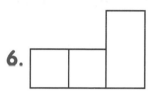

7.

8.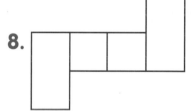

9.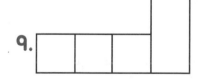

10.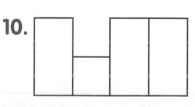

Circle the spelling word in each bigger word.

| steamer | unjust | mustard | bother |
| winner | scoreboard | blend | blast |

# Write It Right

Skills:

Spelling Words
with Final **st**

Words with
**end**

Spelling
Theme
Vocabulary

Spelling Words
in Context

Identifying
Word Families

Circle the correct spelling.

1. I play on the red teem/team.

2. This is our lath/last game.

3. It is the end/ent of the season.

4. Did you see how fast/fest he ran?

5. I can kick the ball with both/bott feet.

6. He can stend/send the ball across the field.

7. Run to the ind/end of the field.

8. Did the blue team scoor/score?

Make word families. Write the words below under the correct heading. Can you add one more word to each family?

| end | cast | dust | bend | mend |
| fast | must | blast | trust | |

| **Last** | **Send** | **Just** |
| --- | --- | --- |
| _____ | _____ | _____ |
| _____ | _____ | _____ |
| _____ | _____ | _____ |
| _____ | _____ | _____ |

# Race Days

> The names of days of the week, months of the year, and holidays begin with capital letters.

On Sunday, we went for a bike ride.

Last June, I saw a bike race.

Jake got a new bike at Christmas.

Read the sentences. Write the words that need a capital letter.

1. We saw a car race on memorial day.

   _____

2. On saturday, we went to the track.

   _____

3. Nick races on sunday night, too.

   _____

4. He came in third on father's day.

   _____

5. Last july, we saw his team race.

   _____

6. Travis came with us thursday night.

   _____

7. Nick's car was fast on friday.

   _____

8. His next race must be in august.

   _____

© Evan-Moor Corp. • EMC 4538 • Spell & Write

**UNIT 3**

**27**

Skills:

Writing
Contractions

Using
Apostrophes

# In the Pool

A contraction is a short way to write two words. A contraction uses an apostrophe ('). The apostrophe takes the place of the missing letter or letters.

| | |
|---|---|
| have not = haven't | I haven't seen you swim. |
| they will = they'll | They'll open the pool at eight o'clock. |
| she had = she'd | Sara said she'd learned how to dive. |

Write the contraction for the two words in blue.

1. I will learn to dive this summer. _____

2. You are a good swimmer. _____

3. Who will show me how to push off? _____

4. She will learn how to swim. _____

5. It should not be hard to learn. _____

6. Do not dive in there. _____

7. That is not the deep end. _____

8. Brent said he would like to swim. _____

9. I am floating. _____

10. We did not dive today. _____

28  UNIT 3

# Here I Go!

> Use **I** when you are the person doing something.
> Use **me** when something happens to you.
>
> **I skate onto the ice.**
> **Dan skates with me.**

Read each sentence. Write **I** or **me** in the blank.

1. _____ like to skate.

2. Mom and _____ went to the ice rink.

3. She helped _____ tie my skates.

4. Other skaters watched out for _____.

5. _____ didn't go fast.

6. Mom showed _____ how to stop on ice.

7. She said _____ skate very well.

8. Now _____ can skate fast.

9. Just watch _____ go!

10. _____ can even twirl!

# I Want to Play!

What sport would you like to play? Write three reasons why you want to play this sport.

I would like to play _____.

Three reasons I want to play this sport are:

**First:** _____

_____

_____

**Second:** _____

_____

_____

**Third:** _____

_____

_____

# Dear Pen Pal...

Skills:

Writing a
Letter

Using Spelling
Words in a
Composition

Your pen pal wants to know what sport you like best. Write a letter.
Tell your pen pal about the sport you like and why you like it. Use
as many spelling words as you can.

_____
date

Dear _____ ,

_____

_____

_____

_____

_____

_____

_____

Your friend,

_____

---

## ✔ Check Your Story

○  I wrote complete sentences.

○  I used my best handwriting.

○  I checked my spelling.

Find the correct answer. Fill in the circle.

1. Which word or words need a capital letter?
   ○ my birthday
   ○ saturday
   ○ this week

2. Which word is a contraction for the two words **what is**?
   ○ who's
   ○ whats
   ○ what's

3. Which sentence uses **I** or **me** correctly?
   ○ Ben and me played ball.
   ○ Ben and I played a game.
   ○ He threw the ball to I.

4. Which sentence has the correct capital letters?
   ○ We saw a game on Thanksgiving Day.
   ○ The pool is open on valentine's day.
   ○ Our team was lucky on st. patrick's day.

## My Spelling Test

Ask someone to test you on the spelling words.

1. _____
2. _____
3. _____
4. _____
5. _____
6. _____
7. _____
8. _____
9. _____
10. _____

5. Write the sentence correctly.

   **our team just couldnt scor on wednesday**

   _____

   _____

# Blue Whales

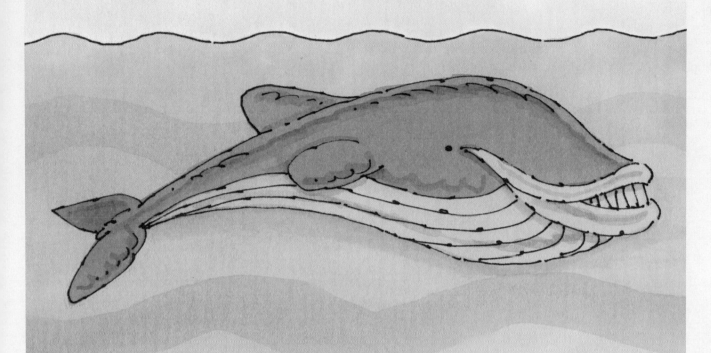

Whales swim in all the Earth's oceans. They can dive deep and stay there for a long time. Whales are very big animals. The blue whale is the biggest animal on Earth. Blue whales are even bigger than the dinosaurs were. They can weigh as much as thirty elephants! The blue whale eats tiny ocean animals called krill. The krill float in the water. A blue whale eats as it swims along. Plates in its jaw trap the krill. The whale's mouth strains out the water and leaves the krill. A blue whale eats about one hundred pounds of food with every gulp.

**Find It!** Read the spelling words.
Check off the words you can find in the story.

- [ ] boat
- [ ] float
- [ ] long
- [ ] along
- [ ] paw
- [ ] jaw
- [ ] belong
- [ ] shark
- [ ] whale
- [ ] swim

How many spelling words did you find? _____

**Skills:**

Spelling Words with **oa**, **ong**, and **aw**

Spelling Theme Vocabulary

Visual Memory

# Spelling Practice

## Read and Spell

## Copy and Spell

## Spell It Again!

1. boat

2. float

3. long

4. along

5. belong

6. jaw

7. paw

8. shark

9. whale

10. swim

# Spelling Time

Fill in all the missing vowels to make spelling words.

| a | e | i | o |

l ____ ng                 al ____ ng

b ____ l ____ ng          wh ____ l ____

b ____ ____ t             f l ____ ____ t

p ____ w                  j ____ w

sw ____ m                 sh ____ rk

Circle two words in each row that rhyme with the first word.

| 1. **float** | coat | toot | boat |
|---|---|---|---|
| 2. **long** | wrong | song | ring |
| 3. **paw** | was | law | jaw |
| 4. **swim** | him | one | trim |
| 5. **sail** | whale | ball | pail |
| 6. **shark** | park | bark | tank |

Skills:

Spelling Words
with **oa**, **ong**,
and **aw**

Spelling
Theme
Vocabulary

Visual Memory

Writing
Complete
Sentences

Spelling in
Context

# Read and Spell

Read each sentence. Unscramble the word in **bold**. Write the
sentence correctly on the line. Circle the spelling word.

1. We took a **toba** ride on the ocean.

   _____

2. We watched for a **wheal**.

   _____

3. What do you think came **agonl**?

   _____

4. We saw a whale **miws** next to us.

   _____

5. It was a very **lnog** animal.

   _____

6. It had a big **wja** and a big tail.

   _____

7. Next time I will look for a **harsk**.

   _____

   _____

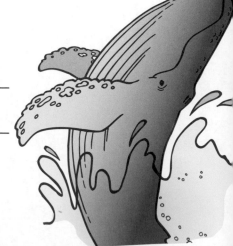

# More Contractions

A contraction is a short way to write two words. A contraction uses an apostrophe. The apostrophe takes the place of the missing letter or letters.

**are not = aren't**

Write the correct contraction in each sentence.

haven't   didn't   isn't   can't   needn't   hadn't   don't

1. I _____ know this aquarium had sharks.
   did not

2. We _____ seen the shark tank yet.
   have not

3. I _____ think this is a shark.
   do not

4. Taylor _____ seen a shark before.
   had not

5. _____ that a shark over there?
   Is not

6. You _____ be afraid.
   need not

7. It _____ swim out of the tank.
   can not

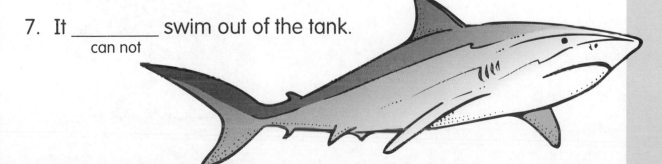

# Is and Are

Use is with one.
Use are with more than one.

> There is a whale out there.
> There are three whales swimming.

Read the sentences. Write **is** or **are** in the blanks.

1. I think sea otters _____ cute.

2. That sea otter _____ looking for lunch.

3. An otter _____ floating on its back.

4. Sea otters _____ fun to watch.

5. Sea otters _____ good at using rocks.

6. Rocks _____ used to open shells.

7. One paw _____ holding a rock.

8. The other paw _____ holding a shell.

9. The otter _____ hitting the shell.

10. Lunch _____ inside!

# Whose Is It?

> **Apostrophes (') are used to show who owns something.**
>
> **The boat belongs to Dan.**
> **Dan's boat is called the *Blue Whale*.**

Read the sentences. Fill in the missing words to show who owns something. Use **'s**.

1. The beach house belongs to Grandpa.

   We are going to _____ beach house.

2. The shells belong to Jada.

   These are _____ shells.

3. That tooth came from a shark.

   That is a _____ tooth.

4. That boat belongs to the neighbor.

   The _____ boat is on the beach.

5. Leo painted a whale picture.

   I like _____ painting.

6. Tera has a new pool.

   Can we swim in _____ pool?

**Skills:**

Prewriting and
Organizing

Writing
Complete
Sentences

# Words About Whales

Fill in the drawing. In each shape, write a word that tells about whales. Then use some of your words to write two sentences about whales.

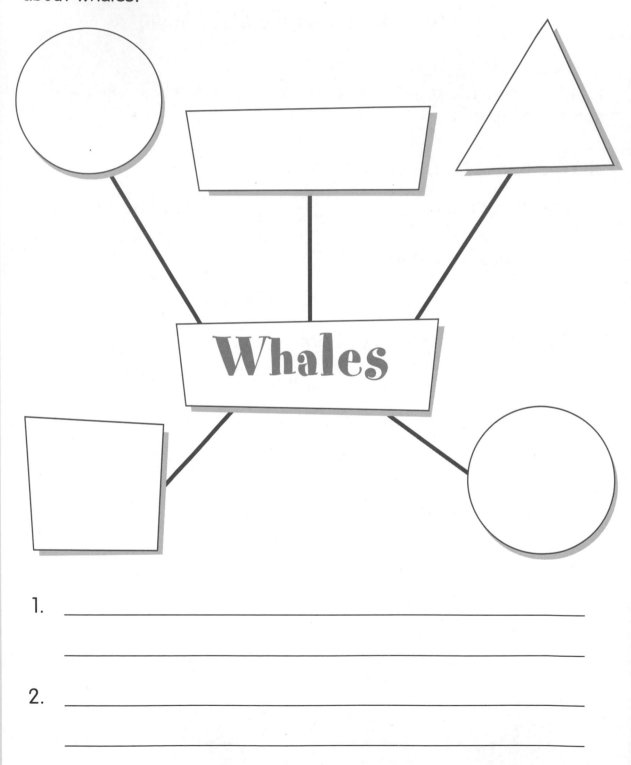

1. _____

_____

2. _____

_____

# A Trip to the Aquarium

Pretend your class went on a trip to an aquarium. You made a scrapbook about it. Draw a photo for your scrapbook. Write about the photo. Use some of your spelling words.

| boat | float | long | along | belong |
|------|-------|------|-------|--------|
| jaw  | paw   | shark | whale | swim  |

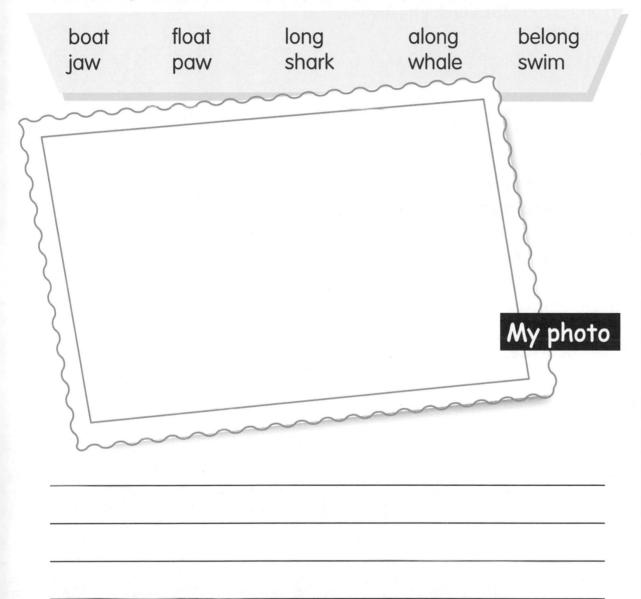

My photo

_____

_____

_____

_____

## ✓ Check Your Story

○ I wrote complete sentences.

○ I checked my spelling.

## Blue Whales

## My Spelling Test

Find the correct answer. Fill in the circle.

1. Which one is a contraction for the two words **did not**?
   - ○ don't
   - ○ didn't
   - ○ didnot

2. Which sentence uses **are** correctly?
   - ○ Whales and sharks are ocean animals.
   - ○ A baby whale are swimming.

3. Which sentence uses **is** correctly?
   - ○ Those otters is playing.
   - ○ The otter is looking for food.

4. Read the sentence. What is the missing word?

   We went sailing in _____ boat.
   - ○ Claire's
   - ○ Claires
   - ○ Claires'

Ask someone to test you on the spelling words.

1. _____

2. _____

3. _____

4. _____

5. _____

6. _____

7. _____

8. _____

9. _____

10. _____

5. Write the sentence correctly.

   the baby wale wont flote aloung with Bens boate

   _____

   _____

Spell & Write • EMC 4538 • © Evan-Moor Corp.

# Rainy Days

Today when I woke up, the sky was blue. It looked like it would be a sunny day. I called my friend Kayla to ask her to come over. She lives across the way. We like to jump rope. When Kayla got here, the sky was cloudy. Before long, it started to rain. So we went inside and played a board game. We wished the rain would stop. In a little while, the rain did stop. We went outside again to jump rope. That's when Kayla spotted a beautiful rainbow. How do you chase away rain clouds? I don't know. But if you wait a little while, you may see a rainbow.

**Find It!** Read the spelling words.
Check off the words you can find in the story.

| | | | | |
|---|---|---|---|---|
| ☐ way | ☐ away | ☐ today | ☐ play | ☐ played |
| ☐ rain | ☐ wait | ☐ chase | ☐ sky | ☐ sunny |

How many spelling words did you find? _____

# Spelling Practice

## Read and Spell | Copy and Spell | Spell It Again!

1. way

2. away

3. today

4. play

5. played

6. rain

7. wait

8. chase

9. sky

10. sunny

# Crossword Fun

Fill in the spelling words to complete the crossword puzzles.

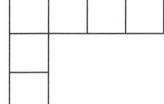

| way | away | today | play | played |
| rain | wait | chase | sky | sunny |

1. [grid of squares]

2. [grid of squares]

3. [grid of squares]

You used six spelling words in the puzzles. Use the other four spelling words in this sentence.

Will the sun c _____ a _____

the r _____ t _____?

# Find the Mistakes

Cross out the misspelled words.

1. waye    way

2. chace    chase

3. played    playd

4. rain    rane

5. uway    away

6. todday    today

7. play    plaiy

8. sky    skie

9. suny    sunny

10. wate    wait

Correct the sentences.

1. Can you plaiy todday?

_____

2. The skie is suny after the rane.

_____

_____

# Windy Weather

> **A sentence begins with a capital letter.**
>
> **Do you think it will rain today?**

Rewrite these sentences. Begin each sentence with a capital letter.

1. it is windy today.

   _____

2. the trees bend way over.

   _____

3. leaves spin in the air.

   _____

4. we chase the leaves.

   _____

5. the flag is flying.

   _____

Draw a picture of a windy day.

# All About Adjectives

**Some words describe nouns. These are called adjectives.**

**white snow     dark clouds     warm wind**

Circle the adjectives in the sentences.

1. I like stormy weather.

2. There was a big storm yesterday.

3. Today is a sunny day.

4. The blue sky is back.

5. We can play in the fluffy white snow.

6. I will put on my new red mittens.

7. The cold air bites my nose.

8. Let's make a funny snowman.

# In the Clouds

▶ Use we when you and other people do something.

Use us when something happens to you and other people.

We watch the weather.
It rained on us.

Fill in the circle by the correct word.

1. On sunny days _____ sit on the grass.   ○ we    ○ us

2. _____ love to watch the clouds.   ○ We    ○ Us

3. Would you like to watch with _____?   ○ we    ○ us

4. Why don't you join _____?   ○ we    ○ us

5. Sometimes _____ see cloud animals.   ○ we    ○ us

6. _____ see them chase each other.   ○ We    ○ Us

7. Look for faces in the clouds with _____.   ○ we    ○ us

8. Are the cloud faces watching _____?   ○ we    ○ us

# Weather Chart

Your class is keeping track of the weather this week. You made a chart. The chart shows if the weather is cloudy or sunny. The numbers tell how warm it is. Read the weather chart. Then write two sentences about the weather this week.

| Monday | Tuesday | Wednesday | Thursday | Friday |
|---|---|---|---|---|
| | | | | |
| cloudy<br>75° | rainy<br>69° | sunny<br>80° | sunny<br>85° | sunny<br>88° |

1. _____

   _____

2. _____

   _____

# Storm in the Sky

Tell about a storm you can remember. Use adjectives to tell about the storm. Use some of your spelling words.

| way | away | today | play | played |
| rain | wait | chase | sky | sunny |

_____

_____

_____

_____

_____

_____

_____

_____

_____

## ✔ Check Your Story

○ I used adjectives.

○ I began each sentence with a capital letter.

○ I checked my spelling.

## My Spelling Test

Find the correct answer. Fill in the circle.

1. Which sentence is correct?
   - ○ Come and play in the rain.
   - ○ the rain has stopped.
   - ○ did you get wet?

2. Which word is an adjective
   (a word that describes a noun)?
   - ○ today
   - ○ sunny
   - ○ chase

3. Which sentence uses **we** correctly?
   - ○ Sam played in the snow with we.
   - ○ May we play in the snow?

4. Which sentence uses **us** correctly?
   - ○ His bike splashed us.
   - ○ Us and Kim splashed in the rain.

Ask someone to test you on the spelling words.

1. _____
2. _____
3. _____
4. _____
5. _____
6. _____
7. _____
8. _____
9. _____
10. _____

5. Write the sentence correctly.

   we had to wate until the rane went uwaye to playe

   _____

   _____

# Time for School

It was a school day. My dog Rex shook the covers to wake me up. I ate a good breakfast. I took the bus to school. Soon I got off the bus. Something was different. My school looked like an old-time school. It was like the little red schoolhouse I had read about in a book. The kids were all dressed funny, too. The teacher looked at me without a smile. She asked for my work. Oh, no! Did I forget my best book report at home? Just then I heard Mom say, "Wake up, it's time for school." I had only been dreaming.

**Find It!**

Read the spelling words.
Check off the words you can find in the story.

| | | | | |
|---|---|---|---|---|
| good | book | took | shook | school |
| soon | too | read | best | work |

How many spelling words did you find? _____

# Spelling Practice

## Read and Spell | Copy and Spell | Spell It Again!

1. good

2. book

3. took

4. shook

5. school

6. soon

7. too

8. read

9. best

10. work

# Sound Search

Cut out the word cards. Read the words. Glue them in the correct boxes.

| Sound of o͞o in room | Sound of o͝o in foot |
|---|---|
| | |
| | |
| | |
| | |
| | |
| | |
| | |
| | |

| | | | |
|---|---|---|---|
| good | book | too | shook |
| wood | shoot | look | pool |
| school | soon | took | zoo |
| noon | hook | boom | cook |

Skills:

Spelling Words
with **oo**

Spelling
Theme
Vocabulary

Visual
Discrimination

Writing a
Complete
Sentence

# Hidden Words

Circle the spelling word in each bigger word. Write the spelling word on the line.

1. notebook _____

2. stool _____

3. good-bye _____

4. bassoon _____

5. mistook _____

6. homework _____

7. numbest _____

8. reader _____

9. preschooler _____

10. shook-up _____

Write a sentence using the words **took** and **book**.

_____

_____

# At the Start

▶ **A sentence begins with a capital letter.**

**School will start again soon.**

Rewrite each sentence. Use a capital letter.

1. our school has a book trade day.

   _____

2. bring in an old book.

   _____

3. you can trade your book.

   _____

4. you can get a good book.

   _____

5. then you can read it.

   _____

6. read it to a friend.

   _____

# Punctuation

A sentence needs ending punctuation.

- A telling sentence ends with a period. (.)
- An asking sentence ends with a question mark. (?)
- A sentence that shows strong feeling ends with an exclamation point. (!)

I go to Red Hill School.

What school do you go to?

That's my school, too!

Write the correct punctuation mark at the end of each sentence.

1. How do you get to school_____

2. Some kids walk to school_____

3. Some ride in a car_____

4. Do you take the bus_____

5. A horse would be fun_____

6. Could you take a boat_____

7. Some kids do_____

8. How about a bike_____

9. We could ride fast_____

10. Hurry, don't be late_____

# They or Them?

Skills:

Using
Pronouns **they**
and **them**

Writing
Complete
Sentences

▶ Use they when several people do something.
Use them when something happens to several people.

They worked on their book reports.
The teacher helped them.

Rewrite the sentences. Use **they** or **them** in place of the underlined names.

1. <u>Kyle and Ben</u> are in my class.

   _____

2. I like to work with <u>Jessica and Mei</u>.

   _____

3. Did <u>Shelby and Kate</u> read the same book?

   _____

4. <u>Robert and Jose</u> are best friends.

   _____

5. I read my book to <u>Sara and Steve</u>.

   _____

6. Let's read <u>Marco and Lin</u> another book.

   _____

# My School

Write complete sentences to answer the questions. Begin each sentence with a capital letter. End it with a punctuation mark.

1. What is the name of your school?

   _____

   _____

2. Where is your school?

   _____

   _____

3. What is the best thing about your school?

   _____

   _____

4. What would you change about your school?

   _____

   _____

Draw a picture of your school.

# My Learning Log

What do you like to learn best in school? Is it reading, writing, or spelling? Is it math, music, science, or something else? Write about it. Tell why you like it. Tell about one thing you have learned. Use some of your spelling words.

| good | book | took | shook | school |
|------|------|------|-------|--------|
| soon | too | read | best | work |

_____

_____

_____

_____

_____

_____

_____

_____

## ✓ Check Your Story

○ I began each sentence with a capital letter.

○ I used a period, question mark, or exclamation point at the end of each sentence.

Find the correct answer. Fill in the circle.

1. Which sentence is correct?
   - ○ i think school is fun.
   - ○ we work at school.
   - ○ They had a good time.

2. Read the sentence. Choose the correct punctuation mark.

   Hooray, our team won____
   - ○ period (.)
   - ○ question mark (?)
   - ○ exclamation point (!)

3. Read the sentence. Choose the correct punctuation mark.

   Who is your teacher____
   - ○ period (.)
   - ○ question mark (?)
   - ○ exclamation point (!)

4. Choose the correct word to complete the sentence.

   _____ took the bus home.
   - ○ They
   - ○ Them
   - ○ Us

Ask someone to test you on the spelling words.

1. _____

2. _____

3. _____

4. _____

5. _____

6. _____

7. _____

8. _____

9. _____

10. _____

5. Write the sentence correctly.

   they tuuk a goode bouk to reed at skool

   _____

   _____

# Class Show

Our class is having a show. Do you know the story about the Three Billy Goats Gruff? They wanted to cross the bridge to eat some grass. I am playing the biggest Billy Goat. The mean troll is no match for me! He jumps off the bridge with a shout. Then the Three Billy Goats Gruff are safe to cross the bridge. We go trip-trap, trip-trap!

We made hats to wear in the show. I had to learn my part. So I read it over and over. Now I know all the words. The show will start when everyone sits down. When the show ends, the players will stand in a row. We will all take a bow. I hope you will like our show.

**Find It!**  Read the spelling words.
Check off the words you can find in the story.

| | | | | |
|---|---|---|---|---|
| ☑ now | ☑ down | ☑ shout | ☑ about | ☑ our |
| ☑ house | ☑ show | ☑ row | ☑ part | ☑ start |

How many spelling words did you find? _____

# Spelling Practice

## Read and Spell | Copy and Spell | Spell It Again!

1. now

2. down

3. shout

4. about

5. our

6. house

7. show

8. row

9. part

10. start

# Search for Sounds

Read each word. Listen to the sound of **ow**.
Then write the word under the correct heading.

| show | now | how | row | down | blow |

| Sound of ow in cow | Sound of ow in slow |
| --- | --- |
| _____ | _____ |
| _____ | _____ |
| _____ | _____ |

Write a spelling word to finish each sentence.

1. The show will _____ at two o'clock.

2. It is _____ the "Three Little Pigs."

3. One little pig made a brick _____.

4. I hope you like _____ show.

# Word Study

Write the letter pairs to finish the spelling words.

| ou | ow | ar |

1.  n_____

2.  h_____se

3.  _____r

4.  ab_____t

5.  d_____n

6.  r_____

7.  p_____t

8.  sh _____t

9.  st_____t

10. sh_____

Cross out the misspelled word in each pair.

1.  down      doun

2.  shout     showt

3.  abowt     about

4.  staret    start

5.  rowe      row

6.  house     howse

7.  nowe      now

8.  part      prat

9.  shou      show

10. owr       our

# Noting Names

> ▶ The names of people, pets, and specific places and things begin with capital letters.

> Will Ann go see the pets on parade?
> Her dog Harry is in the show.
> It is at Pine Park.

Circle the names that need capital letters.

1. oak park school will have a play.

2. The play is called *spring sounds*.

3. We will sing a song about froggy.

4. He asks miss mousie to marry him.

5. The song says she has to ask uncle rat.

6. My sister kim helps me practice.

7. My dog pepper likes to sing with us.

8. pepper likes the song about froggy.

Pepper

# Capital I

Use a capital letter for the word that names yourself—I.

Hanna and I like to dance.

Rewrite each sentence correctly. Watch for the word I.

1. You clap and i sing.

   _____

2. i dance and you swing.

   _____

3. You hop and i tap.

   _____

4. i jump and you rap.

   _____

5. You and i sing high and low.

   _____

6. You and i put on a show.

   _____

# You're Invited

▶ The greeting and closing in a letter begin with a capital letter.

> Dear Miss Mousie,
> Will you marry me?
>
> Love,
> Froggy

Circle the words that need a capital letter.

dear Mom and dad,
We are having a show. please come to school on Friday at two o'clock.
love,
Adam

dear Room 12,
our class is having a play. We hope you can come to see it on Wednesday after lunch.
your friends,
Room 10

dear Grandma,
Can you come to my school on thursday? We are having a puppet show at one o'clock.
yours truly,
Stephanie

# Come to Our Show

Your class is having a music show. Write a letter to invite someone to the show. Use some of your spelling words.

| now | down | shout | about | our |
|------|------|-------|-------|-------|
| house | show | row | part | start |

_____

_____

_____

_____

_____

_____

_____

_____

_____

✔ **Check Your Story**

◯ I used capital letters in the greeting and closing.

◯ I used capital letters to begin names.

# The Players

Your class is putting on a play about Little Red Riding Hood. Write a sentence to tell about the part each child will play. Use a capital letter for each name.

**Emma**        **Gabe**          **Ana**

**Little Red**   **Woodsman**      **Big Bad Wolf**
**Riding Hood**

1. _____

_____

2. _____

_____

3. _____

_____

Skills:

Writing
Complete
Sentences

Using Picture
Clues

Capitalizing
Names

# Class Show

## My Spelling Test

Find the correct answer. Fill in the circle.

1. Which sentence has the correct capital letters?
   - ○ We know a song about Froggy.
   - ○ Who is miss mousie?

2. Which sentence is correct?
   - ○ Can i be the wolf in your play?
   - ○ You and I can be in the show.

3. Which closing has the correct capital letter?
   - ○ yours truly,
   - ○ Your friend,
   - ○ love,

4. Which group of words needs capital letters?
   - ○ little red riding hood
   - ○ school play
   - ○ making puppets

Ask someone to test you on the spelling words.

1. _____

2. _____

3. _____

4. _____

5. _____

6. _____

7. _____

8. _____

9. _____

10. _____

5. Write the sentence correctly.

   i have to stert learning my parte for owr showo

   _____

   _____

# Space Ride

What if we flew into space? Put on your space suit. Five . . . four . . . three . . . two . . . one . . . liftoff! We are flying above the planet Earth. Did you remember to bring food, air, and water? Our first stop is the moon. From here, the Earth looks like a big blue stone. You can see land. You can see lots of water. We can't stay, so get ready for liftoff again. The sun is very far away. It looks like a big orange. It is very hot. Our rocket cannot stand the heat. Let's turn here. Off we go into the Milky Way. Who knows? We may find a new star!

**Find It!**

Read the spelling words.
Check off the words you can find in the story.

| | |
|---|---|
| ☑ stand | ☑ star |
| ☑ ring | ☑ bring |

☑ stand   ☑ star   ☑ stone   ☑ flew   ☑ new

☑ ring   ☑ bring   ☑ moon   ☑ sun   ☑ off

How many spelling words did you find? _____

# Spelling Practice

## Read and Spell

1. stand

2. star

3. stone

4. flew

5. new

6. ring

7. bring

8. moon

9. sun

10. off

## Copy and Spell

_____

_____

_____

_____

_____

_____

_____

_____

_____

_____

## Spell It Again!

_____

_____

_____

_____

_____

_____

_____

_____

_____

_____

# Out in Space

| stand | star | stone | flew | new |
| ring | bring | moon | sun | off |

**Skills:**

Spelling Words Beginning with **st**

Words Ending with **ew** and **ing**

Spelling Theme Vocabulary

Writing Spelling Words

Reading and Understanding Clues

Rhyming Words

Read each clue. Write the spelling word.

1. rhymes with **band** _____

2. a rock _____

3. begins with **r** _____

4. not on _____

5. rhymes with **soon** _____

6. begins with **br** _____

7. rhymes with **fun** _____

8. not old _____

9. begins like **fly** _____

10. rhymes with **jar** _____

© Evan-Moor Corp. • EMC 4538 • Spell & Write

**UNIT 8**

75

Skills:

Spelling Words
Beginning
with **st**

Words Ending
with **ew**
and **ing**

Spelling
Theme
Vocabulary

Visual Memory

# Space Puzzles

Fill in the boxes with the spelling words.

| stand | star | stone | flew | new |
|-------|------|-------|------|-----|
| ring | bring | moon | sun | off |

1.

6.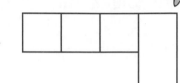

2.

7.

3.

8.

4.

9.

5.

10.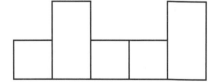

Circle the spelling word in each bigger word.

standing        starlight        birthstone        offer

newt        ringing        moonlight        sunny

# Name the Noun

► **A noun is a word that names a person, place, or thing.**

woman—person
Mars—place
rock—thing

Write each noun under the correct heading.

| stone | space | girl | ring | boy |
| moon | worker | rocket | Earth | |

| Person | Place | Thing |
|--------|-------|-------|
| _____ | _____ | _____ |
| _____ | _____ | _____ |
| _____ | _____ | _____ |

Write a noun in each blank.

1. The _____ went to _____.

2. Then the _____ saw the _____.

# Picking Pronouns

Some words take the place of names (nouns). These words are called pronouns.

she    her    he    him    it    we    us    they    them

Sandy and Tim rode the rocket.

They flew it to the moon.

Rewrite each sentence. Use a pronoun to replace the word or words in color.

1. The sun gives us light.

   _____

2. Matt flew his rocket.

   _____

3. Darius and I saw the moon.

   _____

4. Carol learned about stars.

   _____

5. I want to see the rocket.

   _____

6. Bring the stone to Ali and Sam.

   _____

# Commas in Sentences

Commas are used to separate things in a list.

**I would like to visit the sun, the moon, and Mars.**

Write a sentence using each word list.
Use commas to separate the items.

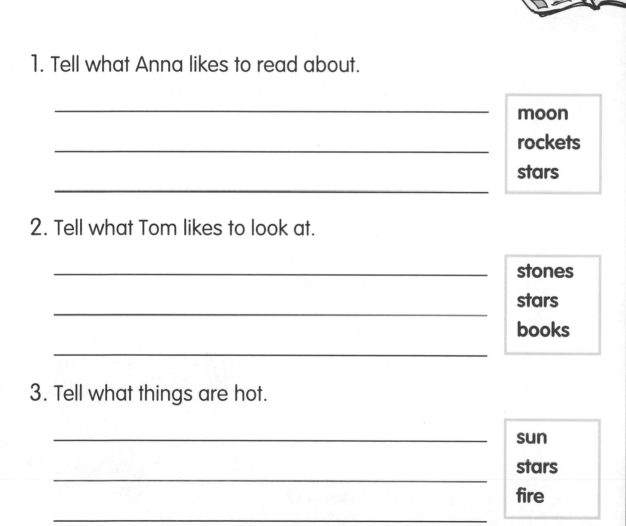

1. Tell what Anna likes to read about.

_____

_____

_____

| moon |
| rockets |
| stars |

2. Tell what Tom likes to look at.

_____

_____

_____

| stones |
| stars |
| books |

3. Tell what things are hot.

_____

_____

_____

| sun |
| stars |
| fire |

# Here We Go!

You are going to take a trip into space. What will you pack to take with you? What things will make you feel at home? Make a list.

1. _____

2. _____

3. _____

4. _____

5. _____

6. _____

7. _____

8. _____

9. _____

10. _____

Write a sentence that tells three things you will bring with you. Use commas in your sentence.

_____

_____

# Visit from Space

Write an ending for the story. Use some of your spelling words.

| stand | star | stone | flew | new |
| ring | bring | moon | sun | off |

I woke up one night and looked out the window. The sky was full of stars. The moon was bright. Just then, a ship from space flew into the yard. It landed without a sound. The door of the ship opened.

_____

_____

_____

_____

_____

_____

_____

_____

✔ **Check Your Story**

○  I wrote complete sentences.
○  I checked my spelling.

# Space Ride

## My Spelling Test

Find the correct answer. Fill in the circle.

1. Which word is a noun?
   - ⭘ flew
   - ⭘ off
   - ⭘ moon

2. Which word is a noun?
   - ⭘ new
   - ⭘ star
   - ⭘ bring

3. Which pronoun can replace the words in bold?

   **Jose and I** read about stars.

   - ⭘ They
   - ⭘ We
   - ⭘ Them

4. Which sentence uses commas correctly?
   - ⭘ I like to draw the sky, stars, and moon.
   - ⭘ We have books about rockets jets, and planes.
   - ⭘ Where are the books, about the Earth sun and, stars?

Ask someone to test you on the spelling words.

1. _____

2. _____

3. _____

4. _____

5. _____

6. _____

7. _____

8. _____

9. _____

10. _____

5. Write the sentence correctly.

   **a noo rocket floo to the moone to breeng a stoan back to Earth**

   _____

   _____

Spell & Write • EMC 4538 • © Evan-Moor Corp.

# All Aboard!

    Have you ever taken a train ride? My dad and I rode the train into the city. Dad said it was Kids' Day at the place where he works. He rides the train to work every day. We took the number nine. It is a fast train. Some trains make a stop along the way. But the number nine does not. First, we passed by houses and trees. Then, we saw the big buildings of the city. My dad works in one of those buildings. The train stopped at the station. We walked from there to Dad's work. It was fun to go to work with Dad. I met lots of nice people. The train trip was fun, too.

**Find It!** Read the spelling words.
Check off the words you can find in the story.

| | | | |
|---|---|---|---|
| ☐ trip | ☐ trees | ☐ train | ☐ stop | ☐ stopped |
| ☐ number | ☐ say | ☐ said | ☐ ride | ☐ fast |

How many spelling words did you find? _____

# Spelling Practice

## Read and Spell | Copy and Spell | Spell It Again!

1. trip

2. trees

3. train

4. stop

5. stopped

6. number

7. say

8. said

9. ride

10. fast

# Rhyme Time

Draw a line to match the words that rhyme.

| | | | |
|---|---|---|---|
| trip | fast | trees | day |
| ride | slide | say | mop |
| brain | red | stopped | bees |
| past | flip | lumber | popped |
| said | stain | stop | number |

Fill in the missing letters.    **st        tr**

1. You are a fa_____ runner.

2. I know how to _____op my bike.

3. Park your bike under the _____ee.

4. The cars _____opped at the light.

5. Look, a _____ain is going by.

6. We are taking a plane _____ip.

# Double It!

Make new words. Double the consonant. Then add ed. This verb tells what already happened.

pop (what is happening)

pop + p + ed = popped (what already happened)

1. stop _____

2. trip _____

3. slip _____

4. rub _____

5. trot _____

Write each group of words in alphabetical order.

| | | |
|---|---|---|
| stopped _____ | train _____ |
| number _____ | ride _____ |
| trees _____ | said _____ |
| fast _____ | stop _____ |
| say _____ | trees _____ |
| trip _____ | ride _____ |

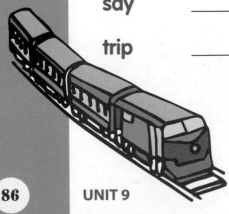

Spell & Write • EMC 4538 • © Evan-Moor Corp.

# Train Trip

▶ The greeting and closing in a letter begin with a capital letter.

Dear Uncle John,
    We are coming to see you on the Fourth of July. Will you meet us at the train station?
                     Love,
                     Owen and Mattie

Circle the words that need a capital letter.

dear Owen and mattie,
    i am glad you are coming. I will meet you at the train station.
               love,
               Uncle john

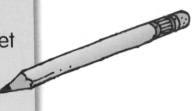

dear Mattie,
    How was your trip? did you take the train? What did you and Owen like best? Please write back.
               your friend,
               Sally

dear Sally,
    We had so much fun! uncle John took us on a river ride! Owen and I got very wet.
           yours truly,
           Mattie

# Car Ride

> Commas are used after the salutation (greeting) and closing in a letter.

Dear Uncle John,
   Thank you for a fun time. We liked the river trip very much. It was wet and wild!
                              Love,
                              Owen and Mattie

Write the commas where they belong.

Dear Sally

   Did you have fun on your car trip? Where did you go? I hope you will tell me about it.

                  Your pal
                  Owen

Dear Owen

   Our car trip was fun. We went to the desert. We saw red rocks. We went camping, too.

                  Your friend
                  Sally

Dear Sally

   Thank you for the postcard. The red rocks are so pretty. I am glad you had fun.

                  Love
                  Ms. May

# Pronoun Puzzler

Some words take the place of names (nouns).
These words are called pronouns.

> she   her   he   him   it   we   us   they   them
>
> **Ben** and I took a boat ride.
>
> The boat brought **us** home.

Read the sentences. Circle the pronoun. Then draw a line from
each pronoun to the noun it replaced.

My family is taking a trip.
We will go on a ship.

The captain says hello.
He shakes my hand.

The ship is very big.
It has two pools.

Mom likes to swim.
She is in the pool.

The ship sails on the ocean.
It is all around the ship.

# Away We Go!

Think about a trip you would like to take. Where would you go?
How would you get there? What would you see?

Make a postcard of your trip. Draw a picture for the front.
Write a note about your trip on the back.

# Magic Train

One day, you got on a magic train. Where did you go? Write a letter to a friend about your trip. Use capital letters and commas in the greeting and closing. Use as many spelling words as you can.

| trip | trees | train | stop | stopped |
|------|-------|-------|------|---------|
| number | say | said | ride | fast |

_____

_____

_____

_____

_____

_____

_____

_____

✔ **Check Your Story**

○ I used a capital letter in the greeting and closing.

○ I used a comma after the greeting and closing.

○ I checked my spelling words.

# All Aboard!

## My Spelling Test

Find the correct answer. Fill in the circle.

1. Which pronoun should replace the words in bold?

    Will you ride in the boat with

    **Hanna and me?**

    ○ we

    ○ they

    ○ us

2. Which greeting has the correct comma?

    ○ Dear, Jose

    ○ Dear Ms. Brown

    ○ Dear Tina,

3. Which closing has the correct capital letter?

    ○ Yours truly,

    ○ sincerely,

    ○ your Friend,

4. Where do you use a greeting and a closing?

    ○ in a story

    ○ in a letter

    ○ in a poem

Ask someone to test you on the spelling words.

1. _____

2. _____

3. _____

4. _____

5. _____

6. _____

7. _____

8. _____

9. _____

10. _____

5. Write the sentence correctly.

    **what is the numbr of the trane you ried home**

    _____

    _____

# The Birthday Party

A birthday party is so much fun! Friends come to the party. They bring presents for the birthday child. They sing the "Happy Birthday" song. Everyone plays games.

There are always good things to eat. The best part is the birthday cake. The birthday child makes a wish and blows out the candles. The wish is supposed to come true if you blow them all out. The cake is cut, and everyone has a big piece. Will there be ice cream, too? Yum!

After the party, the birthday child thanks everyone for coming and for the presents. What a great day!

**Find It!** Read the spelling words.
Check off the words you can find in the story.

| | | | | |
|---|---|---|---|---|
| ☐ cake | ☐ makes | ☐ came | ☐ games | ☐ sing |
| ☐ bring | ☐ presents | ☐ candles | ☐ party | ☐ birthday |

How many spelling words did you find? _____

**Skills:**

Spelling Words with **a-e** and **ing**

Spelling Theme Vocabulary

Visual Memory

| Read and Spell | Copy and Spell | Spell It Again! |
|---|---|---|
| 1. cake | _____ | _____ |
| 2. makes | _____ | _____ |
| 3. came | _____ | _____ |
| 4. games | _____ | _____ |
| 5. sing | _____ | _____ |
| 6. bring | _____ | _____ |
| 7. presents | _____ | _____ |
| 8. candles | _____ | _____ |
| 9. party | _____ | _____ |
| 10. birthday | _____ | _____ |

# Word Puzzles

Skills:

Spelling Words with **a-e** and **Ing**

Spelling Theme Vocabulary

Visual Memory and Discrimination

Word Families

Rhyming Words

Fill in the boxes with the spelling words.

| bring | presents | candles | party |
|-------|----------|---------|-------|
| makes | came | games | sing |

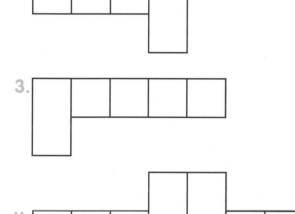

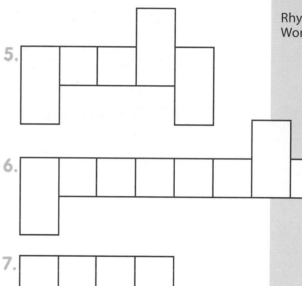

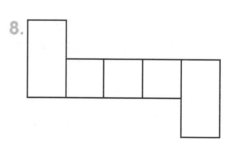

Make word families. Write the words from the word box in the correct box below. Add more words if you can.

| rake | ring | same |
|------|------|------|
| _____ | _____ | _____ |
| _____ | _____ | _____ |
| _____ | _____ | _____ |

bring   game
came   cake
make   sing

Using Context
Clues to
Identify
Missing Words

Writing
Spelling Words

Writing
Complete
Sentences
with Correct
Capitalization
and Ending
Punctuation

# What's Missing?

Fill in the missing spelling words.

| cake | makes | came | games | sing |
|------|-------|------|-------|------|
| bring | presents | candles | party | birthday |

1. Kim was six years old on her _____.

2. Father made a big chocolate _____ for Kim's party.

3. How many guests _____ to the party?

4. They played _____ in the backyard.

5. Let's all _____ "Happy Birthday."

6. Did they bring _____ for the birthday girl?

Write a sentence using each of these spelling words.
Begin with a capital letter. End with correct punctuation.

7. **bring**

   _____

   _____

   _____

8. **candles**

   _____

   _____

   _____

Spell & Write • EMC 4538 • © Evan-Moor Corp.

# Capitals Needed

Sentences begin with a capital letter.

The school bus stops in front of my house.

Names of people and pets begin with a capital letter.

Manuel has a cat named Fluffy.

Circle the words that should begin with a capital letter.
The first one has been done for you.

1. (today) was (kim's) birthday.

2. she had a party.

3. mike, jill, and tammy came to the party.

4. the friends played games.

5. mom gave kim a dog.

6. she named her new dog peewee.

7. jill and tammy gave her a book about cinderella.

8. mike gave kim a big red ball.

9. everybody had fun at kim's party.

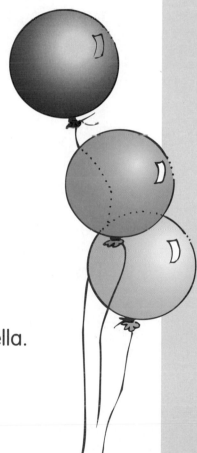

Write a sentence about you and your friends. Use capital letters.

_____

_____

Skills:

Using Correct
Ending
Punctuation

Writing a
Statement,
a Question,
and an
Exclamation

# Make Your Mark

**Use correct punctuation marks at the ends of sentences.**

✓ A telling **sentence** ends with a **period**. (.)

✓ An **asking** sentence ends with a **question mark**. (?)

✓ A sentence that shows strong feeling ends with an **exclamation point**. (!)

Write the correct punctuation at the end of each sentence.

1. May I have a birthday party___

2. Who do you want to invite___

3. Let's play games and eat in the backyard___

4. Dad will cook hot dogs on the grill___

5. Don't touch that hot grill___

6. Are you ready to eat ice cream and cake___

7. Don't drop the birthday cake___

8. Thank you for my presents___

Write a telling sentence.

9. _____

_____

Write an asking sentence.

10. _____

_____

Write a sentence that shows strong feeling.

11. _____

_____

# 1, 2, and 3

> Use a comma (,) between words in a series.
>
> Carlos had a hot dog, chips, and milk for lunch.

Place commas where they are needed.

1. Mother got red green and yellow balloons for the party.

2. Jess asked Tom Jay and Kelly to his birthday party.

3. Is the party on Friday Saturday or Sunday?

4. Did Jess have six seven or eight candles on his cake?

5. Do you want chocolate vanilla or strawberry ice cream with your cake?

6. I decorated the present with blue ribbon a white bow and a gold star.

7. Jess got a bike a football and a game for his birthday.

Write a sentence about a birthday party that lists three things in a series.

_____

_____

_____

_____

# Birthday Questionnaire

Your parents are planning a birthday party for you. Here are some questions they would like you to answer. Write your answers in complete sentences.

1. Where do you want to have your birthday party?

   _____

   _____

2. Who do you want to invite to your party?

   _____

   _____

3. What do you want to eat at your party?

   _____

   _____

4. What games do you want to play at your party?

   _____

   _____

5. How many candles should be on your birthday cake?

   _____

   _____

6. What presents would you like for your birthday?

   _____

   _____

   _____

# A Funny Birthday Party

Write a story about a birthday party for a pet dog named Sam. Use as many spelling words as you can.

| | | | | |
|---|---|---|---|---|
| cake | makes | came | games | sing |
| bring | presents | candles | party | birthday |

_____

_____

_____

_____

_____

_____

_____

_____

_____

_____

## ✔ Check Your Story

○ I wrote complete sentences.

○ I used capital letters where they were needed.

○ I used correct punctuation marks.

## My Spelling Test

Find the correct answer. Fill in the circle.

1. Which punctuation mark goes at the end of the sentence?
   How many children came to the birthday party___
   - ○ period (.)
   - ○ question mark (?)
   - ○ exclamation point (!)

2. Which punctuation mark goes at the end of the sentence?
   That was the best chocolate cake I've ever had___
   - ○ · period (.)
   - ○ question mark (?)
   - ○ exclamation mark (!)

3. Which group of words should begin with a capital letter?
   - ○ a birthday present.
   - ○ they played games at the party.
   - ○ eating birthday cake.

4. Where should the commas go in this sentence?
   Jill Mike and Tammy came to the party.
   - ○ Jill, Mike, and Tammy
   - ○ Jill Mike, and, Tammy
   - ○ Jill, Mike and Tammy

Ask someone to test you on the spelling words.

1. _____
2. _____
3. _____
4. _____
5. _____
6. _____
7. _____
8. _____
9. _____
10. _____

5. Write the sentence correctly.

### did sam bring a presunt to my birthda partee

_____

_____

Spell & Write • EMC 4538 • © Evan-Moor Corp.

# Bunny Puppets

We had fun in art class today. Mrs. Green showed us how to make something new. We made bunny puppets! Here's how to make the puppet. First, paint a stick. Then cut two paper circles. One circle is the head, and one is the body. You could use any color paper you wish. My bunny is brown. Glue the circles to the stick. Then draw two round eyes. Draw a triangle nose. Then make two long ears. Glue them onto the bunny. Put a ball of cotton on the back for a tail. Now, give your bunny a name. I named my bunny Floppy. I can make Floppy hop around.

**Find It!** Read the spelling words.
Check off the words you can find in the story.

- [ ] could
- [ ] would
- [ ] found
- [ ] round
- [ ] around
- [ ] something
- [ ] brown
- [ ] green
- [ ] draw
- [ ] paint

How many spelling words did you find? _____

# Spelling Practice

## Read and Spell | Copy and Spell | Spell It Again!

1. could

2. would

3. found

4. round

5. around

6. something

7. brown

8. green

9. draw

10. paint

# Unscramble and Spell

Read each sentence. Unscramble the spelling word. Write it on the line.

1. ouCld I use your colored pens? _____

2. I ndouf a box of crayons. _____

3. Will you wadr me a picture? _____

4. What loudw you like to draw? _____

5. Next time we can pntai. _____

6. Do you have wnbor paint? _____

7. No, but I have reneg. _____

8. I'll draw a druno ball. _____

Words with **ou**

Spelling
Theme
Vocabulary

Visual Memory

Alphabetical
Order

Writing
Complete
Sentences

# ABC Order

Write the spelling words in alphabetical order.

| green | brown | around | round | draw |
| paint | could | found | would | something |

1. _____     6. _____

2. _____     7. _____

3. _____     8. _____

4. _____     9. _____

5. _____     10. _____

Use the words **draw** and **something** in a sentence.

_____

_____

Use the words **paint** and **green** in a sentence.

_____

_____

A·B·C·D·E·F·G·H·I·J·K

# Color Splash!

> A sentence needs ending punctuation.
>
> • A telling sentence ends with a period. (.)
>
> • An asking sentence ends with a question mark. (?)
>
> • A sentence that shows strong feeling ends with an exclamation point. (!)

Read the story.

Do you like to paint? Tanya loves to paint. Give her a big piece of paper. She will make something with many colors. Splash! Red goes on first. Splat! Next are blue and green. Sploosh! Now, here is some purple and yellow. What do you see? It's a rainbow!

1. Write a telling sentence from the story.

   _____

   _____

2. Write an asking sentence from the story.

   _____

   _____

3. Write three words from the story that show strong feeling.

   _____

   _____

# Mixed-up Adjectives

**Some words describe nouns. These are called adjectives.**

**slimy snakes     green eggs     bright colors**

Finish this silly story. Write an adjective in each sentence. You can even think of your own! Then read your silly story to someone.

| brown | round | red | new |
| tiny | fuzzy | green | funny |

My brother likes to draw _____ dragons.

He doesn't draw _____ ones. The dragons have

_____ eyes. They have _____ tails.

Some wear _____ hats. Some of the dragons

eat _____ ice cream. The dragons sing

_____ songs. They live in _____ houses.

Draw a silly picture to go with your story.

# Artist's Things

> **An apostrophe (') is used to show who owns something.**
>
> **This paint set belongs to Ally.**
> **Ally's paint set is open.**

Read the sentences. Write in the missing word to show who owns something. Use 's.

1. Ms. Brown is the art teacher.

    We are in Ms. _____ class.

2. Tamika made a clay dish.

    _____ dish is pretty.

3. Luke made a mask.

    _____ mask looks like a lion.

4. Rose put her painting outside.

    _____ painting is still wet.

5. Kyle can draw a rocket.

    Did you see _____ rocket?

6. Jarvis makes animals with clay.

    Look at _____ clay animals.

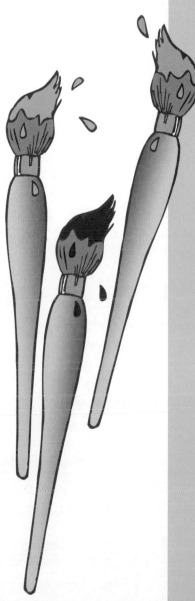

# Picture

_____
(your name + 's)

Draw a picture of yourself. Then write about it below.

I wear _____

My hair _____  My eyes _____

Write three adjectives that tell about you.

_____

_____

_____

# Art Talks

Finish the story. Use some of your spelling words.

| could | would | found | round | around |
|-------|-------|-------|-------|--------|
| something | brown | green | draw | paint |

One day, our teacher took us to see some paintings. I got a big surprise. One painting was of a smiling lady. When I walked by the lady, she said something to me!

_____

_____

_____

_____

_____

_____

_____

_____

_____

## ✔ Check Your Story

○ I wrote complete sentences.

○ I used correct ending punctuation.

○ I checked my spelling.

# Bunny Puppets

## My Spelling Test

Find the correct answer. Fill in the circle.

1. Which sentence has the correct ending punctuation?
   - ○ I like to paint?
   - ○ How did you draw that.
   - ○ Did you use a red crayon?

2. Which sentence has the correct ending punctuation?
   - ○ Don't spill the paint!
   - ○ Where are the brushes.
   - ○ I like your picture?

3. Which word is an adjective?
   - ○ picture
   - ○ green
   - ○ draw

4. Which word describes the underlined word?
   I made a round <u>dish</u> in art class.
   - ○ class
   - ○ made
   - ○ round

Ask someone to test you on the spelling words.

1. _____
2. _____
3. _____
4. _____
5. _____
6. _____
7. _____
8. _____
9. _____
10. _____

5. Write the sentence correctly.

   may I pante grean flowers arownd Amys drawing

   _____

   _____

Spell & Write • EMC 4538 • © Evan-Moor Corp.

# In the Garden

This summer, I have a job. I help my neighbor with her garden. Her name is Mrs. Gomez. Her garden is in pots. The pots are very pretty. Many of them have flowers that bloom. Some of the pots have vegetable plants. I have never planted anything before. Mrs. Gomez gave me a pot with some soil. She helped me plant each seed. I gave them water every day. My plants grew and grew. Now they are tall and green. They have pretty blooms, too. Someday I will have my own garden.

**Find It!**

Read the spelling words.
Check off the words you can find in the story.

- they
- their
- many
- any
- anything
- water
- bloom
- soil
- plant
- seed

How many spelling words did you find? _____

# Spelling Practice

| Read and Spell | Copy and Spell | Spell It Again! |
|---|---|---|
| 1. they | _____ | _____ |
| 2. their | _____ | _____ |
| 3. many | _____ | _____ |
| 4. any | _____ | _____ |
| 5. anything | _____ | _____ |
| 6. water | _____ | _____ |
| 7. bloom | _____ | _____ |
| 8. soil | _____ | _____ |
| 9. plant | _____ | _____ |
| 10. seed | _____ | _____ |

# See and Spell

Practice your spelling words. Write the missing letters.

| **they** | **their** | **many** |
|---|---|---|
| ___ ___ey <br><br> th ___ ___ <br><br> ___ ___ ___ ___ | ___ ___ eir <br><br> th ___ ___ r <br><br> ___ ___ ___ ___ ___ | ___ any <br><br> man ___ <br><br> ___ ___ ___ ___ |

| **any** | | **anything** |
|---|---|---|
| ___ ___y <br><br> a ___ ___ <br><br> ___ ___ ___ | | ___ ___ ___ thing <br><br> any ___ ___ ing <br><br> ___ ___ ___ ___ ___ ___ ___ ___ |

| **water** | **bloom** | **soil** |
|---|---|---|
| ___ ___ ___er <br><br> wat ___ ___ <br><br> ___ ___ ___ ___ ___ | ___ ___oom <br><br> bl ___ ___ m <br><br> ___ ___ ___ ___ ___ | ___oil <br><br> s ___ ___ l <br><br> ___ ___ ___ ___ |

| **plant** | **seed** | |
|---|---|---|
| ___ ___ ant <br><br> pl ___ ___ ___ <br><br> ___ ___ ___ ___ ___ | ___ ee ___ <br><br> s ___ ___ d <br><br> ___ ___ ___ ___ | |

# Growing Words

Choose the correct spelling. Write it on the line.

1. Let's plent/plant a garden. _____

2. You must water/watter it every day. _____

3. Do you have eny/any seeds? _____

4. This soil/sole will grow good plants. _____

5. How meny/many seeds do you want? _____

6. Look at these flowers bloom/blume. _____

Circle each spelling word.

seedplantsoilbloomanywateranythingmanytheirthey

anythingtheirmanyseedanytheywatersoilplantbloom

plantbloomanythingmanytheyseedsoilwateranytheir

# Days, Months, and Holidays

> The names of days of the week, months of the year, and holidays begin with capital letters.
>
> Monday, September 6 is Labor Day.

Write the day, month, or holiday that needs a capital letter.

1. We planted our garden on mother's day.

   _____

2. On saturday we picked weeds.

   _____

3. It is my turn to water on wednesday.

   _____

4. Here is a green flower for st. patrick's day.

   _____

5. Flowers bloom in june.

   _____

6. We gave Grandma some roses on sunday.

   _____

7. In october we will pick pumpkins.

   _____

8. Mom makes pumpkin pie for thanksgiving.

   _____

# Search for Verbs

Verbs are words that tell what is happening or has already happened. They name an action.

They grow cactuses in their garden. (what is happening)

Last year, we grew watermelons. (what already happened)

Color each watering can that names a verb.

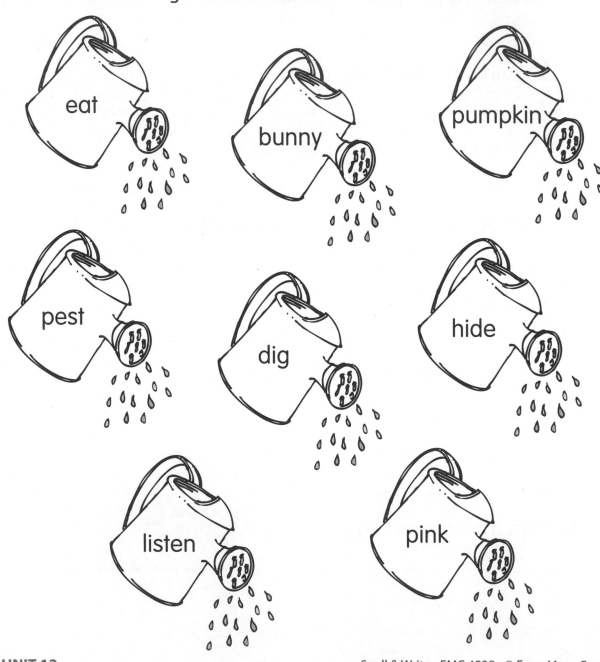

eat

bunny

pumpkin

pest

dig

hide

listen

pink

# Commas Here and There

▶ Commas are used in dates.

### August 7, 2005

Look at a calendar. Write the date for each holiday this year. Put a comma in the date.

Valentine's Day     _____

Mother's Day     _____

Memorial Day     _____

Father's Day     _____

Labor Day     _____

St. Patrick's Day     _____

▶ Commas are used in addresses.

### Salem, Oregon

Write each address. Write a comma between the name of the city and the state or country.

Paris France     _____

Detroit Michigan     _____

Tampa Florida     _____

Toronto Ontario     _____

Dallas Texas     _____

Venice Italy     _____

Florida

Skills:

Writing
Information

Writing
Complete
Sentences

# Garden Calendar

Keisha and her dad are making a garden plan. Look at the calendar. Write three sentences telling about their plan.

| | MAY | | | | | |
|---|---|---|---|---|---|---|
| | 1 Start seeds in cups | 2 | 3 | 4 | 5 | 6 |
| 7 | 8 | 9 Turn the soil | 10 | 11 | 12 | 13 |
| 14 | 15 | 16 | 17 | 18 Plant | 19 the pumpkins | 20 |
| 21 Trim the roses | 22 | 23 | 24 | 25 | 26 | 27 |
| 28 | 29 | 30 | 31 Pick the cherries | | | |

1. _____

   _____

2. _____

   _____

3. _____

   _____

# Our Garden

Look at this picture. Write three sentences about the picture. Use your spelling words.

| they | their | many | any | anything |
|------|-------|------|-----|----------|
| water | bloom | soil | plant | seed |

1. _____

   _____

2. _____

   _____

3. _____

   _____

### ✔ Check Your Story

○ I wrote complete sentences.

○ I used correct ending punctuation.

○ I checked my spelling.

## In the Garden

Find the correct answer. Fill in the circle.

1. Which sentence has the correct capital letters?
   - ◯ Did you pick flowers on monday or tuesday?
   - ◯ Each Friday in June, we go to the garden store.

2. Which sentence has the correct capital letters?
   - ◯ I put candy on the Christmas tree.
   - ◯ These flowers are for mother's day.

3. Which word is a verb?
   - ◯ seeds
   - ◯ planted
   - ◯ any

4. Which date has the correct comma?
   - ◯ January 6, 2005
   - ◯ April, 26 1999
   - ◯ October 31 2007,

## My Spelling Test

Ask someone to test you on the spelling words.

1. _____

2. _____

3. _____

4. _____

5. _____

6. _____

7. _____

8. _____

9. _____

10. _____

5. Write the sentence correctly.

meny people plante flowers so thay bloum in august

_____

_____

| Unit | Test Page | Topic | Test Your Skills Score (5 possible) | Spelling Test Score (10 possible) |
|---|---|---|---|---|
| 1 | 12 | A Good Pet | | |
| 2 | 22 | Busy Bees | | |
| 3 | 32 | At the Gym | | |
| 4 | 42 | Blue Whales | | |
| 5 | 52 | Rainy Days | | |
| 6 | 62 | Time for School | | |
| 7 | 72 | Class Show | | |
| 8 | 82 | Space Ride | | |
| 9 | 92 | All Aboard! | | |
| 10 | 102 | The Birthday Party | | |
| 11 | 112 | Bunny Puppets | | |
| 12 | 122 | In the Garden | | |

# Pull-out Spelling Lists

Use these lists to give spelling tests, to post on the refrigerator, and for extra practice.

| Unit 1<br>A Good Pet | Unit 2<br>Busy Bees | Unit 3<br>At the Gym |
|---|---|---|
| 1. came | 1. she | 1. send |
| 2. name | 2. he | 2. end |
| 3. ride | 3. got | 3. both |
| 4. bone | 4. see | 4. fast |
| 5. cute | 5. bee | 5. last |
| 6. mine | 6. queen | 6. must |
| 7. dog | 7. hive | 7. just |
| 8. cat | 8. sting | 8. team |
| 9. bird | 9. fly | 9. win |
| 10. pet | 10. buzz | 10. score |

# Pull-out Spelling Lists

Use these lists to give spelling tests, to post on the refrigerator, and for extra practice.

| Unit 4<br>Blue Whales | Unit 5<br>Rainy Days | Unit 6<br>Time for School |
|---|---|---|
| 1. boat | 1. way | 1. good |
| 2. float | 2. away | 2. book |
| 3. long | 3. today | 3. took |
| 4. along | 4. play | 4. shook |
| 5. belong | 5. played | 5. school |
| 6. jaw | 6. rain | 6. soon |
| 7. paw | 7. wait | 7. too |
| 8. shark | 8. chase | 8. read |
| 9. whale | 9. sky | 9. best |
| 10. swim | 10. sunny | 10. work |

# Pull-out Spelling Lists

Use these lists to give spelling tests, to post on the refrigerator, and for extra practice.

| Unit 7 Class Show | Unit 8 Space Ride | Unit 9 All Aboard! |
|---|---|---|
| 1. now | 1. stand | 1. trip |
| 2. down | 2. star | 2. trees |
| 3. shout | 3. stone | 3. train |
| 4. about | 4. flew | 4. stop |
| 5. our | 5. new | 5. stopped |
| 6. house | 6. ring | 6. number |
| 7. show | 7. bring | 7. say |
| 8. row | 8. moon | 8. said |
| 9. part | 9. sun | 9. ride |
| 10. start | 10. off | 10. fast |

# Pull-out Spelling Lists

Use these lists to give spelling tests, to post on the refrigerator, and for extra practice.

| Unit 10 The Birthday Party | Unit 11 Bunny Puppets | Unit 12 In the Garden |
|---|---|---|
| 1. cake | 1. could | 1. they |
| 2. makes | 2. would | 2. their |
| 3. came | 3. found | 3. many |
| 4. games | 4. round | 4. any |
| 5. sing | 5. around | 5. anything |
| 6. bring | 6. something | 6. water |
| 7. presents | 7. brown | 7. bloom |
| 8. candles | 8. green | 8. soil |
| 9. party | 9. draw | 9. plant |
| 10. birthday | 10. paint | 10. seed |

# Answer Key

## Page 3

**A Good Pet**

My sister has a new pet. Can you guess what it is? It is not a dog, a cat, or a bird. It is a pet she can ride. It's a pony!

The pony has a white star on her nose. My sister gave her the name Star. Star is a cute pony. Although she is full-grown, she is little. Sometimes I help my sister feed and brush Star. We keep her stall clean, too. Sometimes my sister lets me ride her pony. When I brought an apple for Star, she came to me. Star is a good pet. I hope that someday I will have a pony of my own.

**Find It!** Read the spelling words. Check off the words you can find in the story.

✓ came ✓ name ✓ ride ☐ bone ✓ cute
☐ mine ✓ dog ✓ cat ✓ bird ✓ pet

How many spelling words did you find? **8**

## Page 5

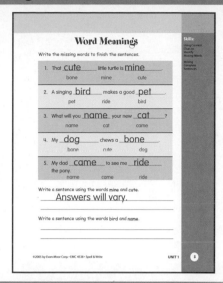

**Word Meanings**

Skills: Using Context Clues to Identify Missing Words; Writing Complete Sentences

Write the missing words to finish the sentences.

1. That **cute** little turtle is **mine**.
   bone · mine · cute

2. A singing **bird** makes a good **pet**.
   pet · ride · bird

3. What will you **name** your new **cat**?
   name · cat · came

4. My **dog** chews a **bone**.
   bone · ride · dog

5. My dad **came** to see me **ride** the pony.
   came · ride

Write a sentence using the words mine and cute.
**Answers will vary.**

Write a sentence using the words bird and name.

## Page 6

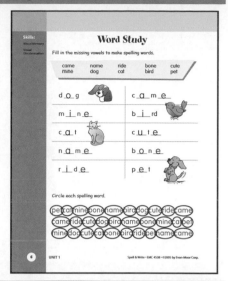

**Word Study**

Skills: Visual Memory; Visual Discrimination

Fill in the missing vowels to make spelling words.

| came | name | dog | ride | bone | cute |
| mine | dog | cat | bird | pet |

d o g    c a m e
m i n e    b i r d
c a t    c u t e
n a m e    b o n e
r i d e    p e t

Circle each spelling word.

pet cat mine bone name bird dog cute ride came
came ride cute dog bird name bone mine cat pet
mine dog cute cat bone bird ride pet name came

## Page 7

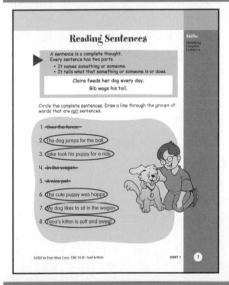

**Reading Sentences**

Skills: Identifying Complete Sentences

A sentence is a complete thought. Every sentence has two parts.
• It names something or someone.
• It tells what that something or someone is or does.

Claire feeds her dog every day.
Bib wags his tail.

Circle the complete sentences. Draw a line through the groups of words that are not sentences.

1. ~~Over the fence.~~
2. (The dog jumps for the ball)
3. (Jake took his puppy for a ride)
4. ~~In the wagon.~~
5. ~~A nice pet~~
6. (The cute puppy was happy)
7. (My dog likes to sit in the wagon)
8. (Tana's kitten is soft and sweet)

## Page 8

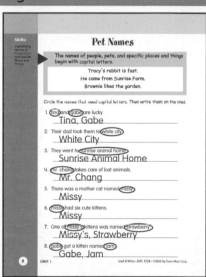

**Pet Names**

Skills: Capitalizing Names of People, Pets, and Specific Places and Things

The names of people, pets, and specific places and things begin with capital letters.

Tracy's rabbit is fast.
He came from Sunrise Farm.
Brownie likes the garden.

Circle the names that need capital letters. Then write them on the lines.

1. (Tina) and (gabe) are lucky.
   **Tina, Gabe**
2. Their dad took them to (white city).
   **White City**
3. They went to (sunrise animal home).
   **Sunrise Animal Home**
4. (mr. chang) takes care of lost animals.
   **Mr. Chang**
5. There was a mother cat named (missy).
   **Missy**
6. (missy) had six cute kittens.
   **Missy**
7. One of (missy's) kittens was named (strawberry).
   **Missy's, Strawberry**
8. (gabe) got a kitten named (jam).
   **Gabe, Jam**

## Page 9

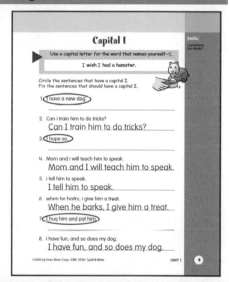

**Capital I**

Skills: Capitalizing the Word I

Use a capital letter for the word that names yourself—I.
I wish I had a hamster.

Circle the sentences that have a capital I. Fix the sentences that should have a capital I.

1. (I have a new dog.)
2. Can i train him to do tricks?
   **Can I train him to do tricks?**
3. (I hope so.)
4. Mom and i will teach him to speak.
   **Mom and I will teach him to speak.**
5. i tell him to speak.
   **I tell him to speak.**
6. when he barks, i give him a treat.
   **When he barks, I give him a treat.**
7. (I hug him and pat him.)
8. i have fun, and so does my dog.
   **I have fun, and so does my dog.**

## Page 10

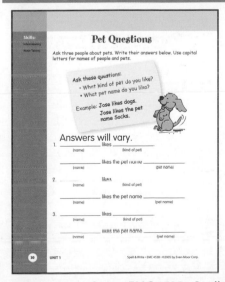

**Pet Questions**

Skills: Interviewing; Note-Taking

Ask three people about pets. Write their answers below. Use capital letters for names of people and pets.

Ask these questions:
• What kind of pet do you like?
• What pet name do you like?

Example: Jose likes dogs.
Jose likes the pet name Socks.

**Answers will vary.**

1. _____ likes _____
   (name)        (kind of pet)
   _____ likes the pet name _____
   (name)                    (pet name)

2. _____ likes _____
   (name)        (kind of pet)
   _____ likes the pet name _____
   (name)                    (pet name)

3. _____ likes _____
   (name)        (kind of pet)
   _____ likes the pet name _____
   (name)                    (pet name)

## Page 11

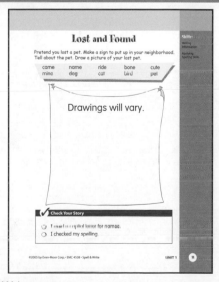

**Lost and Found**

Skills: Writing Information; Applying Spelling Skills

Pretend you lost a pet. Make a sign to put up in your neighborhood. Tell about the pet. Draw a picture of your lost pet.

| came | name | ride | bone | cute |
| mine | dog | cat | bird | pet |

**Drawings will vary.**

✓ Check Your Story
☐ I used a capital letter for names.
☐ I checked my spelling.

## Page 12

**SKILLS    A Good Pet**

Find the correct answer. Fill in the circle.

1. Which group of words is a complete sentence?
   ○ A cute dog.
   ○ Your new kitten.
   ● We found a lost dog.

2. Which sentence has the correct capital letters?
   ○ My horse daisy is a good jumper.
   ● Travis trained his dog Tucker to roll over.
   ○ I like your pet skunk twinkle.

3. Which sentence has the correct capital letter?
   ○ You and i like cats.
   ● Mom said I may feed the fish.
   ○ May I walk the dog?

4. Which sentence needs a capital letter?
   ○ The brown and white dog is mine.
   ● I think rex wants a bone.
   ○ Here is a bone for your dog.

5. Write the sentence correctly.
   i think we should nam that lute bird princess
   **I think we should name that cute bird Princess.**

**My Spelling Test**

Ask someone to test you on the spelling words.

1. _____
2. _____
3. _____
4. _____
5. _____
6. _____
7. _____
8. _____
9. _____
10. _____

## Page 13

### Busy Bees

Did you know that bees have special jobs? The queen bee only has one job. She lays eggs. But worker bees do different jobs as they grow. A worker bee's first job is to clean the hive. When a worker bee is three days old, its body makes food. It feeds the unborn baby bees. Many days later, the worker bee begins to make wax. The wax is used to build new honeycomb cells.

Next, the bee becomes a guard. Guards watch over the hive. They sting bears or people who try to get the hive's honey. When it is three weeks old, the bee must fly away from the hive. All alone, it looks for food in fields and flowers. Worker bees have a busy life!

**Find It!** Read the spelling words. Check off the words you can find in the story.

- ☑ she
- ☐ he
- ☐ got
- ☑ see
- ☑ bee
- ☑ queen
- ☑ hive
- ☑ sting
- ☑ fly
- ☐ buzz

How many spelling words did you find? __6__

## Page 15

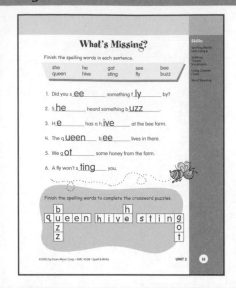

### What's Missing?

Finish the spelling words in each sentence.

| she | he | got | see | bee |
| queen | hive | sting | fly | buzz |

1. Did you s**ee** _____ something f**ly** _____ by?
2. S**he** _____ heard something b**uzz** _____.
3. H**e** _____ has a h**ive** _____ at the bee farm.
4. The q**ueen** _____ b**ee** _____ lives in there.
5. We g**ot** _____ some honey from the farm.
6. A fly won't s**ting** _____ you.

Finish the spelling words to complete the crossword puzzles.

```
b        h
queen hive sting
u              o
z              t
z
```

## Page 16

### Spell and Write

Circle the misspelled words. Write them correctly on the lines.

1. I see Grandma holding a pie. → see
2. Shee put the pie in the window. → She
3. I saw a bee flie by the pie. → fly
4. The bee went buzzz. → buzz
5. The dog got the bee. → got
6. And hee also got the pie. → he

Unscramble the spelling words and write them correctly.

| ebe | qeenu |
| --- | --- |
| bee | queen |
| evih | tgins |
| hive | sting |

## Page 17

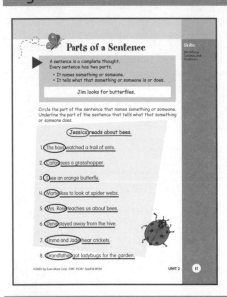

### Parts of a Sentence

A sentence is a complete thought. Every sentence has two parts.
- It names something or someone.
- It tells what that something or someone is or does.

(Jim) looks for butterflies.

Circle the part of the sentence that names something or someone. Underline the part of the sentence that tells what that something or someone does.

(Jessica) reads about bees.

1. (The boys) watched a trail of ants.
2. (Carlos) sees a grasshopper.
3. (I) see an orange butterfly.
4. (Marti) likes to look at spider webs.
5. (Mrs. Rose) teaches us about bees.
6. (Dena) stayed away from the hive.
7. (Emma and Jade) hear crickets.
8. (Grandfather) got ladybugs for the garden.

## Page 18

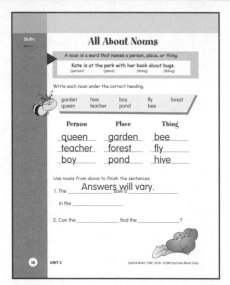

### All About Nouns

A noun is a word that names a person, place, or thing.

Kate is at the park with her book about bugs.
(person) (place) (thing) (thing)

Write each noun under the correct heading.

| garden | hive | boy | fly | forest |
| queen | teacher | pond | bee | |

| Person | Place | Thing |
| --- | --- | --- |
| queen | garden | bee |
| teacher | forest | fly |
| boy | pond | hive |

Use nouns from above to finish the sentences.

1. The _____ Answers will vary. saw a _____
   in the _____.
2. Can the _____ find the _____?

## Page 19

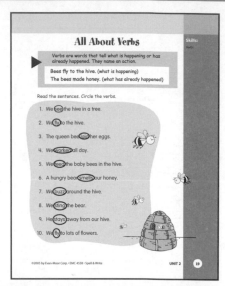

### All About Verbs

Verbs are words that tell what is happening or has already happened. They name an action.

Bees fly to the hive. (what is happening)
The bees made honey. (what has already happened)

Read the sentences. Circle the verbs.

1. We (see) the hive in a tree.
2. We (fly) to the hive.
3. The queen bee (laid) her eggs.
4. We (worked) all day.
5. We (feed) the baby bees in the hive.
6. A hungry bear (smells) our honey.
7. We (buzz) around the hive.
8. We (sting) the bear.
9. He (stays) away from our hive.
10. We (fly) to lots of flowers.

## Page 20

### A New Bug

You just discovered a new kind of bug! Answer the questions about your bug. Then draw a picture of your bug on the leaf.

1. What is your bug's name?
   Answers will vary.
2. What size and shape is your bug?
3. What color is your bug?
4. Where does your bug live?
5. How does your bug get around?
6. What is special about your bug?

## Page 21

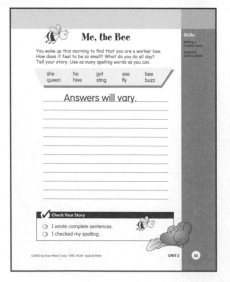

### Me, the Bee

You woke up this morning to find that you are a worker bee. How does it feel to be so small? What do you do all day? Tell your story. Use as many spelling words as you can.

| she | he | got | see | bee |
| queen | hive | sting | fly | buzz |

Answers will vary.

**✓ Check Your Story**
- ○ I wrote complete sentences.
- ○ I checked my spelling.

## Page 22

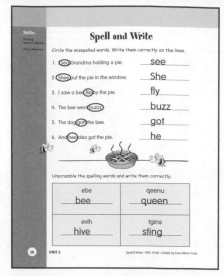

**TEST YOUR SKILLS** — Busy Bees | My Spelling Test

Find the correct answer. Fill in the circle.

1. Read this sentence:
   The boys read a butterfly book.
   Which part names someone?
   ● The boys
   ○ read a butterfly book.

2. Read this sentence:
   My friend Parker likes ladybugs.
   Which part tells what someone does?
   ○ My friend Parker
   ● likes ladybugs.

3. Which word is a noun?
   ○ see
   ○ got
   ● bee

4. Which word is a verb?
   ● work
   ○ hive
   ○ queen

5. Write the sentence correctly.
   hee can hear a bea bozz near the hiv
   He can hear a bee buzz near the hive.

My Spelling Test
Ask someone to test you on the spelling words.

1. _____
2. _____
3. _____
4. _____
5. _____
6. _____
7. _____
8. _____
9. _____
10. _____

**134**

Spell & Write • EMC 4538 • © Evan-Moor Corp.

## Page 23

**At the Gym**

On Saturday, I go to the gym. My friend Amy and I both go there. Last week, we had fun in class. We started with warm-ups. Then we got into teams. Our team wanted to win. We lined up. I put a beanbag on my head. I had to walk from one end of the gym to the other. I got a score of two points. Amy was the next one in line. She put the beanbag on her head. She walked from one end to the other. Our team was fast, but we didn't win this time.

Next, we learned how to make a bridge. You must bend your back and look at the sky. We did log rolls, too. Just hold your arms together over your head. Then roll across the mat. Amy and I will practice at home.

**Find It!** Read the spelling words. Check off the words you can find in the story.

☑ send  ☑ end  ☑ both  ☑ fast  ☑ last
☑ must  ☑ just  ☑ team  ☑ win  ☐ score

How many spelling words did you find? **9**

## Page 25

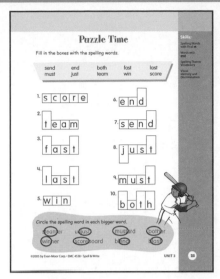

**Puzzle Time**

Fill in the boxes with the spelling words.

send  end  both  fast  last
must  just  team  win  score

1. s c o r e
2. t e a m
3. f a s t
4. l a s t
5. w i n
6. e n d
7. s e n d
8. j u s t
9. m u s t
10. b o t h

Circle the spelling word in each bigger word.

steamer  unjust  mustard  bother
winner  scoreboard  bend  blast

## Page 26

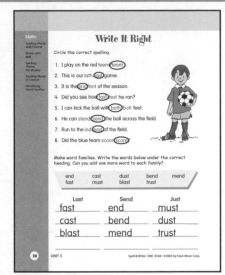

**Write It Right**

Circle the correct spelling.

1. I play on the red team (team).
2. This is our last (last) game.
3. It is the (end) of the season.
4. Did you see how (fast) he ran?
5. I can kick the ball with (both) feet.
6. He can stand (send) the ball across the field.
7. Run to the (end) of the field.
8. Did the blue team scoor (score)?

Make word families. Write the words below under the correct heading. Can you add one more word to each family?

end   cast   dust   bend
fast   must   blast   trust   mend

| Last | Send | Just |
|------|------|------|
| fast | end | must |
| cast | bend | dust |
| blast | mend | trust |

## Page 27

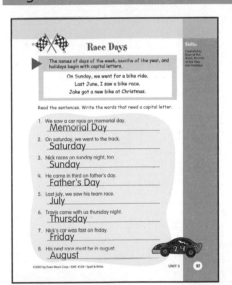

**Race Days**

The names of days of the week, months of the year, and holidays begin with capital letters.

On Sunday, we went for a bike ride.
Last June, I saw a bike race.
Jake got a new bike at Christmas.

Read the sentences. Write the words that need a capital letter.

1. We saw a car race on memorial day. **Memorial Day**
2. On saturday, we went to the track. **Saturday**
3. Nick races on sunday night, too. **Sunday**
4. He came in third on father's day. **Father's Day**
5. Last july, we saw his team race. **July**
6. Travis came with us thursday night. **Thursday**
7. Nick's car was fast on friday. **Friday**
8. His next race must be in august. **August**

## Page 28

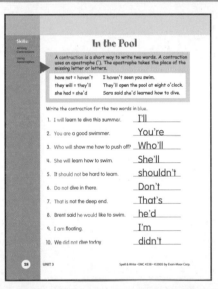

**In the Pool**

A contraction is a short way to write two words. A contraction uses an apostrophe ('). The apostrophe takes the place of the missing letter or letters.

have not = haven't    I haven't seen you swim.
they will = they'll    They'll open the pool at eight o'clock.
she had = she'd    Sara said she'd learned how to dive.

Write the contraction for the two words in blue.

1. I will learn to dive this summer. **I'll**
2. You are a good swimmer. **You're**
3. Who will show me how to push off? **Who'll**
4. She will learn how to swim. **She'll**
5. It should not be hard to learn. **shouldn't**
6. Do not dive in there. **Don't**
7. That is not the deep end. **That's**
8. Brent said he would like to swim. **he'd**
9. I am floating. **I'm**
10. We did not dive today. **didn't**

## Page 29

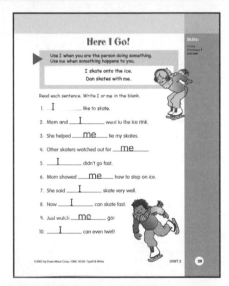

**Here I Go!**

Use I when you are the person doing something. Use me when something happens to you.

I skate onto the ice.
Dan skates with me.

Read each sentence. Write I or me in the blank.

1. **I** like to skate.
2. Mom and **I** went to the ice rink.
3. She helped **me** tie my skates.
4. Other skaters watched out for **me**.
5. **I** didn't go fast.
6. Mom showed **me** how to stop on ice.
7. She said **I** skate very well.
8. Now **I** can skate fast.
9. Just watch **me** go!
10. **I** can even twirl!

## Page 30

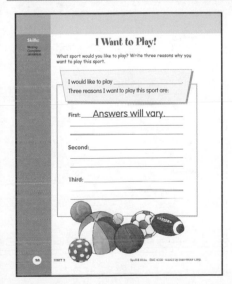

**I Want to Play!**

What sport would you like to play? Write three reasons why you want to play this sport.

I would like to play _____
Three reasons I want to play this sport are:

First: **Answers will vary.**

Second: _____

Third: _____

## Page 31

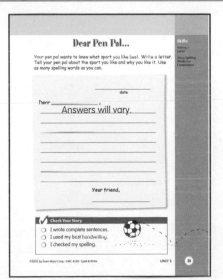

**Dear Pen Pal...**

Your pen pal wants to know what sport you like best. Write a letter. Tell your pen pal about the sport you like and why you like it. Use as many spelling words as you can.

date _____
Dear _____,
**Answers will vary.**

Your friend,

**Check Your Story**
○ I wrote complete sentences.
○ I used my best handwriting.
○ I checked my spelling.

## Page 32

**SKILLS** **At the Gym**

Find the correct answer. Fill in the circle.

1. Which word or words need a capital letter?
   ○ my birthday
   ● saturday
   ○ this week

2. Which word is a contraction for the two words what is?
   ○ who's
   ○ whats
   ● what's

3. Which sentence uses I or me correctly?
   ○ Ben and me played ball.
   ● Ben and I played a game.
   ○ He threw the ball to I.

4. Which sentence has the correct capital letters?
   ● We saw a game on Thanksgiving Day.
   ○ The pool is open on valentine's day.
   ○ Our team was lucky on st. patrick's day.

5. Write the sentence correctly.
   our team just couldnt scor on wednesday
   **Our team just couldn't score on Wednesday.**

**My Spelling Test**

Ask someone to test you on the spelling words.

1. _____
2. _____
3. _____
4. _____
5. _____
6. _____
7. _____
8. _____
9. _____
10. _____

## Page 33

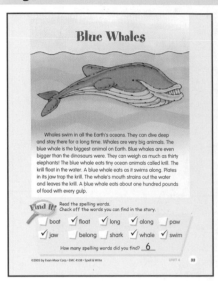

### Blue Whales

Whales swim in all the Earth's oceans. They can dive deep and stay there for a long time. Whales are very big animals. The blue whale is the biggest animal on Earth. Blue whales are even bigger than the dinosaurs were. They can weigh as much as thirty elephants! The blue whale eats tiny ocean animals called krill. The krill float in the water. A blue whale eats as it swims along. Plates in its jaw trap the krill. The whale's mouth strains out the water and leaves the krill. A blue whale eats about one hundred pounds of food with every gulp.

**Find It!** Read the spelling words. Check off the words you can find in the story.

- ☐ boat
- ✓ float
- ✓ long
- ✓ along
- ☐ paw
- ✓ jaw
- ☐ belong
- ☐ shark
- ✓ whale
- ✓ swim

How many spelling words did you find? __6__

## Page 35

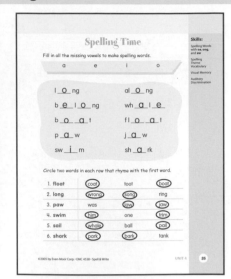

### Spelling Time

Fill in all the missing vowels to make spelling words.

a　e　i　o

l_o_ng　　al_o_ng
b_e_l_o_ng　　wh_a_l_e_
b_o_ _a_t　　fl_o_ _a_t
p_a_w　　j_a_w
sw_i_m　　sh_a_rk

Circle two words in each row that rhyme with the first word.

1. float　(coat)　toot　(boat)
2. long　(wrong)　(song)　ring
3. paw　was　(law)　(jaw)
4. swim　(him)　one　(trim)
5. sail　(whale)　ball　(pail)
6. shark　(park)　(bark)　tank

## Page 36

### Read and Spell

Read each sentence. Unscramble the word in bold. Write the sentence correctly on the line. Circle the spelling word.

1. We took a **toba** ride on the ocean.
   We took a (boat) ride on the ocean.
2. We watched for a **wheal**.
   We watched for a (whale)
3. What do you think came **agonl**?
   What do you think came (along)
4. We saw a whale **miws** next to us.
   We saw a whale (swim) next to us.
5. It was a very **lnog** animal.
   It was a very (long) animal.
6. It had a big **wja** and a big tail.
   It had a big (jaw) and a big tail.
7. Next time I will look for a **harsk**.
   Next time I will look for a (shark)

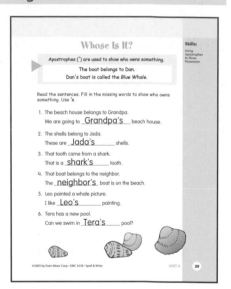

## Page 37

### More Contractions

A contraction is a short way to write two words. A contraction uses an apostrophe. The apostrophe takes the place of the missing letter or letters.

are not = aren't

Write the correct contraction in each sentence.

haven't　didn't　isn't　can't　needn't　hadn't　don't

1. I _didn't_ know this aquarium had sharks.
   did not
2. We _haven't_ seen the shark tank yet.
   have not
3. I _don't_ think this is a shark.
   do not
4. Taylor _hadn't_ seen a shark before.
   had not
5. _Isn't_ that a shark over there?
   Is not
6. You _needn't_ be afraid.
   need not
7. It _can't_ swim out of the tank.
   can not

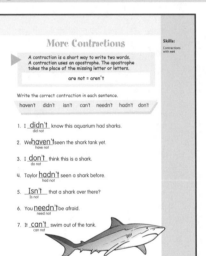

## Page 38

### Is and Are

Use **is** with one.
Use **are** with more than one.

There is a whale out there.
There are three whales swimming.

Read the sentences. Write **is** or **are** in the blanks.

1. I think sea otters _are_ cute.
2. That sea otter _is_ looking for lunch.
3. An otter _is_ floating on its back.
4. Sea otters _are_ fun to watch.
5. Sea otters _are_ good at using rocks.
6. Rocks _are_ used to open shells.
7. One paw _is_ holding a rock.
8. The other paw _is_ holding a shell.
9. The otter _is_ hitting the shell.
10. Lunch _is_ inside!

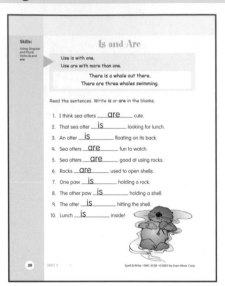

## Page 39

### Whose Is It?

Apostrophes (') are used to show who owns something.

The boat belongs to Dan.
Dan's boat is called the *Blue Whale*.

Read the sentences. Fill in the missing words to show who owns something. Use **'s**.

1. The beach house belongs to Grandpa.
   We are going to _Grandpa's_ beach house.
2. The shells belong to Jada.
   These are _Jada's_ shells.
3. That tooth came from a shark.
   That is a _shark's_ tooth.
4. That boat belongs to the neighbor.
   The _neighbor's_ boat is on the beach.
5. Leo painted a whale picture.
   I like _Leo's_ painting.
6. Tera has a new pool.
   Can we swim in _Tera's_ pool?

## Page 40

### Words About Whales

Fill in the drawing. In each shape, write a word that tells about whales. Then use some of your words to write two sentences about whales.

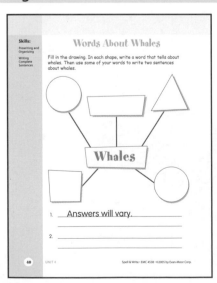

**Whales**

1. _Answers will vary._
2.

## Page 41

### A Trip to the Aquarium

Pretend your class went on a trip to an aquarium. You made a scrapbook about it. Draw a photo for your scrapbook. Write about the photo. Use some of your spelling words.

boat　float　long　along　belong
jaw　paw　shark　whale　swim

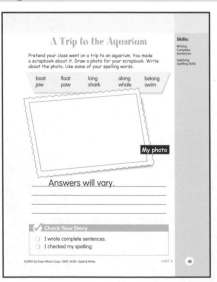

My photo

_Answers will vary._

**✓ Check Your Story**
- ○ I wrote complete sentences.
- ○ I checked my spelling.

## Page 42

### TEST YOUR SKILLS — Blue Whales　　My Spelling Test

Find the correct answer. Fill in the circle.

1. Which one is a contraction for the two words **did not**?
   - ○ don't
   - ● didn't
   - ○ didnot
2. Which sentence uses **are** correctly?
   - ● Whales and sharks are ocean animals.
   - ○ A baby whale are swimming.
3. Which sentence uses **is** correctly?
   - ○ Those otters is playing.
   - ● The otter is looking for food.
4. Read the sentence. What is the missing word?
   We went sailing in ____ boat.
   - ● Claire's
   - ○ Claires
   - ○ Claires'
5. Write the sentence correctly.
   the baby wale wont flote along with Bens boate
   The baby whale won't float along with Ben's boat.

Ask someone to test you on the spelling words.

1. _____
2. _____
3. _____
4. _____
5. _____
6. _____
7. _____
8. _____
9. _____
10. _____

Spell & Write • EMC 4538 • © Evan-Moor Corp.

## Page 43

### Rainy Days

Today when I woke up, the sky was blue. It looked like it would be a sunny day. I called my friend Kayla to ask her to come over. She lives across the way. We like to jump rope. When Kayla got here, the sky was cloudy. Before long, it started to rain. So we went inside and played a board game. We wished the rain would stop. In a little while, the rain did stop. We went outside again to jump rope. That's when Kayla spotted a beautiful rainbow. How do you chase away rain clouds? I don't know. But if you wait a little while, you may see a rainbow.

**Find It!** Read the spelling words. Check off the words you can find in the story.

☑ way  ☑ away  ☑ today  ☐ play  ☑ played
☑ rain  ☑ wait  ☑ chase  ☑ sky  ☑ sunny

How many spelling words did you find? _9_

©2005 by Evan-Moor Corp. • EMC 4538 • Spell & Write        UNIT 5    43

## Page 45

### Crossword Fun

Skills: Spelling Words with ay and ai / Spelling Theme Vocabulary / Visual Memory

Fill in the spelling words to complete the crossword puzzles.

| way | away | today | play | played |
| rain | wait | chase | sky | sunny |

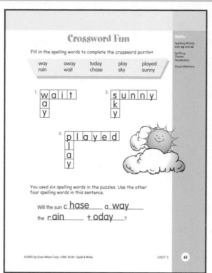

1. w a i t
   a
   y

2. s u n n y
   k
   y

3. p l a y e d
   l
   a
   y

You used six spelling words in the puzzles. Use the other four spelling words in this sentence.

Will the sun c **hase** a **way**
the r **ain** t **oday** ?

©2005 by Evan-Moor Corp. • EMC 4538 • Spell & Write        UNIT 5    45

## Page 46

Skills: Spelling Words with ay and ai / Spelling Theme Vocabulary / Visual Memory

### Find the Mistakes

Cross out the misspelled words.

1. ~~wa~~    way        6. ~~today~~    today
2. ~~chas~~  chase      7. ~~plae~~     play
3. played   ~~plad~~    8. ~~ski~~      sky
4. rain     ~~rane~~    9. ~~suny~~     sunny
5. ~~uwa~~   away       10. ~~wat~~     wait

Correct the sentences.

1. Can you plaiy todday?
   **Can you play today?**

2. The skie is suny after the rane.
   **The sky is sunny after the rain.**

©2005 by Evan-Moor Corp.    UNIT 5        Spell & Write • EMC 4538 • ©2005 by Evan-Moor Corp.    46

## Page 47

### Windy Weather

Skills: Capitalizing the First Word in a Sentence

A sentence begins with a capital letter.

Do you think it will rain today?

Rewrite these sentences. Begin each sentence with a capital letter.

1. it is windy today.
   **It is windy today.**

2. the trees bend way over.
   **The trees bend way over.**

3. leaves spin in the air.
   **Leaves spin in the air.**

4. we chase the leaves.
   **We chase the leaves.**

5. the flag is flying.
   **The flag is flying.**

Draw a picture of a windy day.

©2005 by Evan-Moor Corp. • EMC 4538 • Spell & Write        UNIT 5    47

## Page 48

Skills: Identifying Adjectives

### All About Adjectives

Some words describe nouns. These are called adjectives.

| white snow | dark clouds | warm wind |

Circle the adjectives in the sentences.

1. I like (stormy) weather.
2. There was a (big) storm yesterday.
3. Today is a (sunny) day.
4. The (blue) sky is back.
5. We can play in the (fluffy) (white) snow.
6. I will put on my (new) (red) mittens.
7. The (cold) air bites my nose.
8. Let's make a (funny) snowman.

48    UNIT 5        Spell & Write • EMC 4538 • ©2005 by Evan-Moor Corp.

## Page 49

### In the Clouds

Skills: Using Pronouns we and us

Use we when you and other people do something.
Use us when something happens to you and other people.

We watch the weather.
It rained on us.

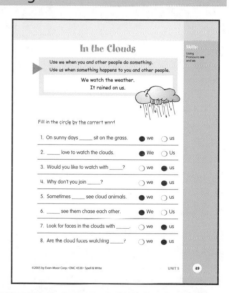

Fill in the circle by the correct word.

1. On sunny days _____ sit on the grass.        ● we  ○ us
2. _____ love to watch the clouds.              ● We  ○ Us
3. Would you like to watch with _____?          ○ we  ● us
4. Why don't you join _____?                    ○ we  ● us
5. Sometimes _____ see cloud animals.           ● we  ○ us
6. _____ see them chase each other.             ● We  ○ Us
7. Look for faces in the clouds with _____.      ○ we  ● us
8. Are the cloud faces watching _____?          ○ we  ● us

©2005 by Evan-Moor Corp. • EMC 4538 • Spell & Write        UNIT 5    49

## Page 50

Skills: Interpreting and Writing Information from a Chart

### Weather Chart

Your class is keeping track of the weather this week. You made a chart. The chart shows if the weather is cloudy or sunny. The numbers tell how warm it is. Read the weather chart. Then write two sentences about the weather this week.

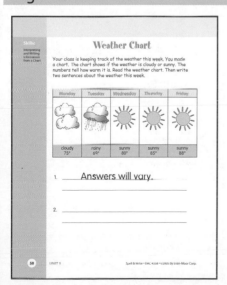

| Monday | Tuesday | Wednesday | Thursday | Friday |
|--------|---------|-----------|----------|--------|
| cloudy | rainy | sunny | sunny | sunny |
| 75° | 69° | 80° | 85° | 88° |

1. **Answers will vary.**

2.

50    UNIT 5        Spell & Write • EMC 4538 • ©2005 by Evan-Moor Corp.

## Page 51

### Storm in the Sky

Skills: Descriptive Writing / Using Adjectives / Applying Spelling Skills

Tell about a storm you can remember. Use adjectives to tell about the storm. Use some of your spelling words.

| way | away | today | play | played |
| rain | wait | chase | sky | sunny |

**Answers will vary.**

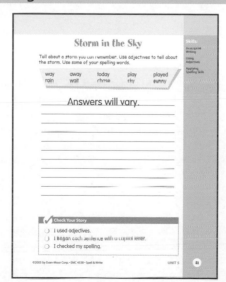

✓ **Check Your Story**
○ I used adjectives.
○ I began each sentence with a capital letter.
○ I checked my spelling.

©2005 by Evan-Moor Corp. • EMC 4538 • Spell & Write        UNIT 5    51

## Page 52

**TEST YOUR SKILLS**   Rainy Days        My Spelling Test

Find the correct answer. Fill in the circle.

1. Which sentence is correct?
   ● Come and play in the rain.
   ○ The rain has stopped.
   ○ did you get wet?

2. Which word is an adjective (a word that describes a noun)?
   ○ today
   ● sunny
   ○ chase

3. Which sentence uses we correctly?
   ○ Sam played in the snow with we.
   ● May we play in the snow?

4. Which sentence uses us correctly?
   ● His hike splashed us.
   ○ Us and Kim splashed in the rain.

5. Write the sentence correctly.
   we had to wate until the rane went awaye to playe
   **We had to wait until the rain**
   **went away to play.**

Ask someone to test you on the spelling words.

1.
2.
3.
4.
5.
6.
7.
8.
9.
10.

52    ASSESSMENT 5        Spell & Write • EMC 4538 • ©2005 by Evan-Moor Corp.

**Time for School**

It was a school day. My dog Rex shook the covers to wake me up. I ate a good breakfast. I took the bus to school. Soon I got off the bus. Something was different. My school looked like an old-time school. It was like the little red schoolhouse I had read about in a book. The kids were all dressed funny, too. The teacher looked at me without a smile. She asked for my work. Oh, no! Did I forget my best book report at home? Just then I heard Mom say, "Wake up, it's time for school." I had only been dreaming.

**Find It!** Read the spelling words. Check off the words you can find in the story.

✓ good ✓ book ☐ took ✓ shook ✓ school
✓ soon ✓ too ✓ read ✓ best ☐ work

How many spelling words did you find? 9

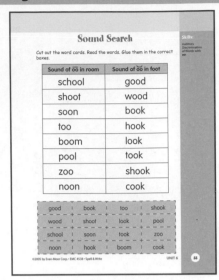

**Sound Search**

Cut out the word cards. Read the words. Glue them in the correct boxes.

| Sound of oo in room | Sound of oo in foot |
|---|---|
| school | good |
| shoot | wood |
| soon | book |
| too | hook |
| boom | look |
| pool | took |
| zoo | shook |
| noon | cook |

| good | book | too | shook |
| wood | shoot | look | pool |
| school | soon | took | zoo |
| noon | hook | boom | cook |

*Skills: Auditory Discrimination of Words with oo*

**Hidden Words**

Circle the spelling word in each bigger word. Write the spelling word on the line.

1. note**book** — book
2. **too** — too
3. **good**bye — good
4. bar**soon** — soon
5. mis**took** — took
6. home**work** — work
7. num**best** — best
8. **read**er — read
9. pre**school**er — school
10. **shook**-up — shook

Write a sentence using the words took and book.
Answers will vary.

*Skills: Spelling Words with oo / Spelling Theme Vocabulary / Visual Discrimination / Writing a Complete Sentence*

**At the Start**

A sentence begins with a capital letter.
School will start again soon.

Rewrite each sentence. Use a capital letter.

1. our school has a book trade day.
Our school has a book trade day.
2. bring in an old book.
Bring in an old book.
3. you can trade your book.
You can trade your book.
4. you can get a good book.
You can get a good book.
5. then you can read it.
Then you can read it.
6. read it to a friend.
Read it to a friend.

*Skills: Capitalizing the First Word in a Sentence*

**Punctuation**

A sentence needs ending punctuation.
• A telling sentence ends with a period. (.)
• An asking sentence ends with a question mark. (?)
• A sentence that shows strong feeling ends with an exclamation point. (!)

I go to Red Hill School.
What school do you go to?
That's my school, too!

Write the correct punctuation mark at the end of each sentence.

1. How do you get to school ?
2. Some kids walk to school .
3. Some ride in a car .
4. Do you take the bus ?
5. A horse would be fun . or !
6. Could you take a boat ?
7. Some kids do . or !
8. How about a bike ?
9. We could ride fast ! or .
10. Hurry, don't be late ! or .

*Skills: Using Ending Punctuation*

**They or Them?**

Use they when several people do something.
Use them when something happens to several people.

They worked on their book reports.
The teacher helped them.

Rewrite the sentences. Use they or them in place of the underlined names.

1. Kyle and Ben are in my class.
They are in my class.
2. I like to work with Jessica and Mei.
I like to work with them.
3. Did Shelby and Kate read the same book?
Did they read the same book?
4. Robert and Jose are best friends.
They are best friends.
5. I read my book to Sara and Steve.
I read my book to them.
6. Let's read Marco and Lin another book.
Let's read them another book.

*Skills: Using Pronouns they and them / Writing Complete Sentences*

**My School**

Write complete sentences to answer the questions. Begin each sentence with a capital letter. End it with a punctuation mark.

1. What is the name of your school?
Answers will vary.
2. Where is your school?
3. What is the best thing about your school?
4. What would you change about your school?

Draw a picture of your school.

*Skills: Writing Complete Sentences*

**My Learning Log**

What do you like to learn best in school? Is it reading, writing, or spelling? Is it math, music, science, or something else? Write about it. Tell why you like it. Tell about one thing you have learned. Use some of your spelling words.

| good | book | took | shook | school |
| soon | too | read | best | work |

Answers will vary.

✓ **Check Your Story**
☐ I began each sentence with a capital letter.
☐ I used a period, question mark, or exclamation point at the end of each sentence.

*Skills: Writing a Personal Narrative*

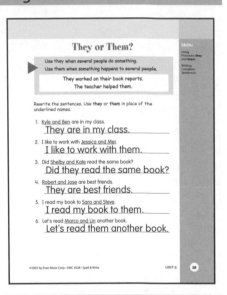

**TEST YOUR SKILLS — Time for School** | **My Spelling Test**

Find the correct answer. Fill in the circle.

1. Which sentence is correct?
○ i think school is fun.
○ we work at school.
● They had a good time.

2. Read the sentence. Choose the correct punctuation mark.
Hooray, our team won___
○ period (.)
○ question mark (?)
● exclamation point (!)

3. Read the sentence. Choose the correct punctuation mark.
Who is your teacher___
○ period (.)
● question mark (?)
○ exclamation point (!)

4. Choose the correct word to complete the sentence.
___ took the bus home.
● They
○ Them
○ Us

5. Write the sentence correctly.
they tuuk a goode bouk to reed at skool
They took a good book to read at school.

Ask someone to test you on the spelling words.
1.
2.
3.
4.
5.
6.
7.
8.
9.
10.

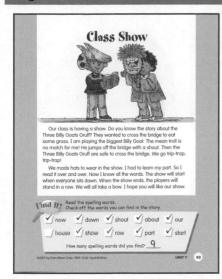

**Class Show**

Our class is having a show. Do you know the story about the Three Billy Goats Gruff? They wanted to cross the bridge to eat some grass. I am playing the biggest Billy Goat. The mean troll is no match for me! He jumps off the bridge with a shout. Then the Three Billy Goats Gruff are safe to cross the bridge. We go trip-trap, trip-trap!

We made hats to wear in the show. I had to learn my part. So I read it over and over. Now I know all the words. The show will start when everyone sits down. When the show ends, the players will stand in a row. We will all take a bow. I hope you will like our show.

**Find It!** Read the spelling words. Check off the words you can find in the story.

- ✓ now  ✓ down  ✓ shout  ✓ about  ✓ our
- ☐ house  ✓ show  ✓ row  ✓ part  ✓ start

How many spelling words did you find? __9__

---

**Search for Sounds**

Read each word. Listen to the sound of *ow*. Then write the word under the correct heading.

| show | now | how | row | down | blow |

| Sound of ow in cow | Sound of ow in slow |
|---|---|
| now | show |
| how | row |
| down | blow |

Write a spelling word to finish each sentence.

1. The show will __start__ at two o'clock.
2. It is __about__ the "Three Little Pigs."
3. One little pig made a brick __house__
4. I hope you like __our__ show.

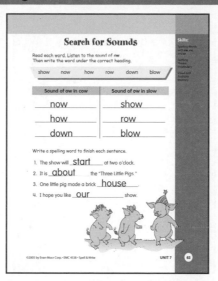

---

**Word Study**

Write the letter pairs to finish the spelling words.

| ou | ow | ar |

1. n__ow__       6. r__ow__
2. h__ou__se     7. p__ar__t
3. __ou__r       8. sh__ou__t
4. ab__ou__t     9. st__ar__t
5. d__ow__n      10. sh__ow__

Cross out the misspelled word in each pair.

1. down ~~dowg~~       6. house ~~hows~~
2. shout ~~showt~~     7. ~~naow~~ now
3. ~~abowt~~ about     8. part ~~pert~~
4. ~~stort~~ start     9. ~~shoe~~ show
5. ~~rou~~ row         10. ~~owr~~ our

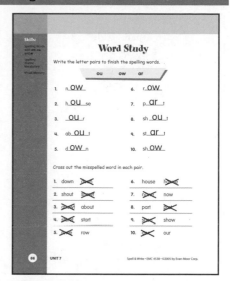

---

**Noting Names**

The names of people, pets, and specific places and things begin with capital letters.

> Will Ann go see the pets on parade?
> Her dog Harry is in the show.
> It is at Pine Park.

Circle the names that need capital letters.

1. (pine park school) will have a play.
2. The play is called (spring sounds)
3. We will sing a song about (froggy)
4. He asks (miss mousie) to marry him.
5. The song says she has to ask (uncle rat)
6. My sister (kim) helps me practice.
7. My dog (pepper) likes to sing with us.
8. (pepper) likes the song about (froggy)

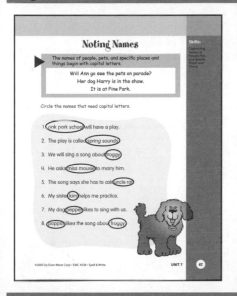

---

**Capital I**

Use a capital letter for the word that names yourself—I.

> Hanna and I like to dance.

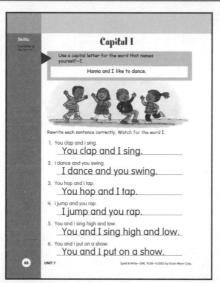

Rewrite each sentence correctly. Watch for the word I.

1. You clap and i sing.
   You clap and I sing.
2. i dance and you swing.
   I dance and you swing.
3. You hop and i tap.
   You hop and I tap.
4. i jump and you rap.
   I jump and you rap.
5. You and i sing high and low.
   You and I sing high and low.
6. You and i put on a show.
   You and I put on a show.

---

**You're Invited**

The greeting and closing in a letter begin with a capital letter.

> Dear Miss Mousie,
> Will you marry me?
>              Love,
>              Froggy

Circle the words that need a capital letter.

(dear) Mom and (dad),
We are having a show. (please) come to school on Friday at two o'clock.
(love),
Adam

(dear) Room 12,
(our) class is having a play. We hope you can come to see it on Wednesday after lunch.
(your) friends,
Room 10

(dear) Grandma,
Can you come to my school on (thursday)? We are having a puppet show at one o'clock.
(yours) truly,
Stephanie

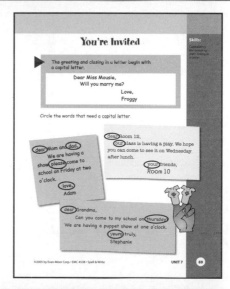

---

**Come to Our Show**

Your class is having a music show. Write a letter to invite someone to the show. Use some of your spelling words.

| now | down | shout | about | our |
| house | show | row | part | start |

Answers will vary.

**✓ Check Your Story**
- ☐ I used capital letters in the greeting and closing.
- ☐ I used capital letters to begin names.

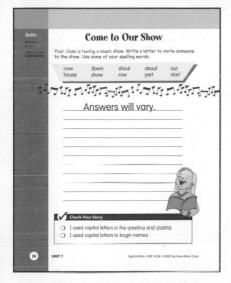

---

**The Players**

Your class is putting on a play about Little Red Riding Hood. Write a sentence to tell about the part each child will play. Use a capital letter for each name.

| Emma | Gabe | Ana |
| Little Red Riding Hood | Woodsman | Big Bad Wolf |

1. Answers will vary.
2.
3.

---

**TEST YOUR SKILLS  Class Show**          **My Spelling Test**

Find the correct answer. Fill in the circle.          Ask someone to test you on the spelling words.

1. Which sentence has the correct capital letters?
   ● We know a song about Froggy.
   ○ Who is miss mousie?

2. Which sentence is correct?
   ○ Can i be the wolf in your play?
   ● You and I can be in the show.

3. Which closing has the correct capital letter?
   ○ yours truly,
   ● Your friend,
   ○ love,

4. Which group of words needs capital letters?
   ● little red riding hood
   ○ school play
   ○ making puppets

1. _____
2. _____
3. _____
4. _____
5. _____
6. _____
7. _____
8. _____
9. _____
10. _____

5. Write the sentence correctly.
   i have to start learning my parte for owr show.
   I have to start learning my part for our show.

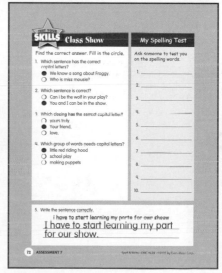

---

## Space Ride

What if we flew into space? Put on your space suit. Five . . . four . . . three . . . two . . . one . . . liftoff! We are flying above the planet Earth. Did you remember to bring food, air, and water? Our first stop is the moon. From here, the Earth looks like a big blue stone. You can see land. You can see lots of water. We can't stay, so get ready for liftoff again. The sun is very far away. It looks like a big orange. It is very hot. Our rocket cannot stand the heat. Let's turn here. Off we go into the Milky Way. Who knows? We may find a new star!

**Find It!** Read the spelling words. Check off the words you can find in the story.

- ✓ stand ✓ star ✓ stone ✓ flew ✓ new
- ☐ ring ✓ bring ✓ moon ✓ sun ✓ off

How many spelling words did you find? __9__

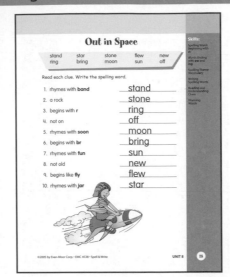

## Out in Space

| stand | star | stone | flew | new |
| ring | bring | moon | sun | off |

Read each clue. Write the spelling word.

1. rhymes with **band** — stand
2. a rock — stone
3. begins with **r** — ring
4. not on — off
5. rhymes with **soon** — moon
6. begins with **br** — bring
7. rhymes with **fun** — sun
8. not old — new
9. begins like **fly** — flew
10. rhymes with **jar** — star

Skills: Spelling Words Beginning with st / Words Ending with sw and ing / Spelling Theme Vocabulary / Writing Spelling Words / Reading and Understanding Clues / Rhyming Words

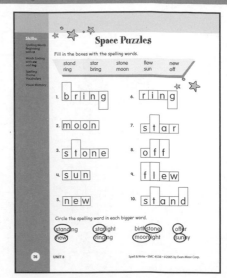

Skills: Spelling Words Beginning with st / Words Ending with sw and ing / Spelling Theme Vocabulary / Visual Memory

## Space Puzzles

Fill in the boxes with the spelling words.

| stand | star | stone | flew | new |
| ring | bring | moon | sun | off |

1. b r i n g
2. m o o n
3. s t o n e
4. s u n
5. n e w
6. r i n g
7. s t a r
8. o f f
9. f l e w
10. s t a n d

Circle the spelling word in each bigger word.

- (stand)ing   (star)light   birth(stone)   (off)er
- (new)   (ring)ing   (moon)light   (sun)ny

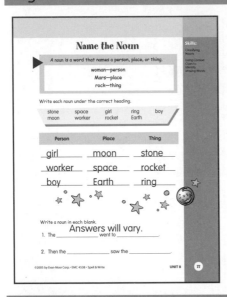

## Name the Noun

A noun is a word that names a person, place, or thing.

woman—person
Mars—place
rock—thing

Write each noun under the correct heading.

| stone | space | girl | ring | boy |
| moon | worker | rocket | Earth |

| Person | Place | Thing |
|--------|-------|-------|
| girl | moon | stone |
| worker | space | rocket |
| boy | Earth | ring |

Write a noun in each blank.

1. The __Answers will vary.__ went to ___
2. Then the ___ saw the ___

Skills: Classifying Nouns / Using Context Clues to Identify Missing Words

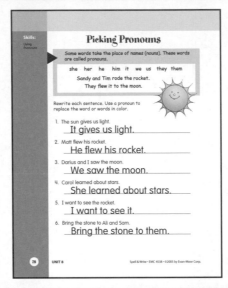

Skills: Using Pronouns

## Picking Pronouns

Some words take the place of names (nouns). These words are called pronouns.

she   her   he   him   it   we   us   they   them

Sandy and Tim rode the rocket.
They flew it to the moon.

Rewrite each sentence. Use a pronoun to replace the word or words in color.

1. The sun gives us light.
   It gives us light.
2. Matt flew his rocket.
   He flew his rocket.
3. Darius and I saw the moon.
   We saw the moon.
4. Carol learned about stars.
   She learned about stars.
5. I want to see the rocket.
   I want to see it.
6. Bring the stone to Ali and Sam.
   Bring the stone to them.

## Commas in Sentences

Commas are used to separate things in a list.

I would like to visit the sun, the moon, and Mars.

Write a sentence using each word list. Use commas to separate the items.

1. Tell what Anna likes to read about.
   Answers will vary.

   | moon |
   | rockets |
   | stars |

2. Tell what Tom likes to look at.

   | stones |
   | stars |
   | books |

3. Tell what things are hot.

   | sun |
   | stars |
   | fire |

Skills: Using Commas in a List

Skills: Writing a List / Using Commas in a List

## Here We Go!

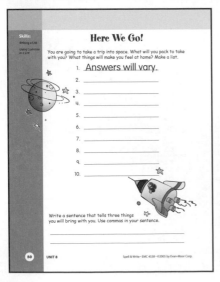

You are going to take a trip into space. What will you pack to take with you? What things will make you feel at home? Make a list.

1. Answers will vary.
2.
3.
4.
5.
6.
7.
8.
9.
10.

Write a sentence that tells three things you will bring with you. Use commas in your sentence.

## Visit from Space

Write an ending for the story. Use some of your spelling words.

| stand | star | stone | flew | new |
| ring | bring | moon | sun | off |

I woke up one night and looked out the window. The sky was full of stars. The moon was bright. Just then, a ship from space flew into the yard. It landed without a sound. The door of the ship opened.

Answers will vary.

Skills: Writing a Creative Ending to a Story

✓ **Check Your Story**
- ○ I wrote complete sentences.
- ○ I checked my spelling.

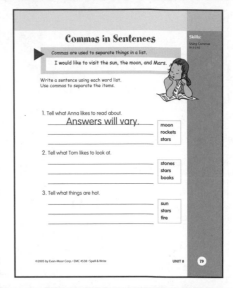

**TEST YOUR SKILLS**   Space Ride     My Spelling Test

Find the correct answer. Fill in the circle.

1. Which word is a noun?
   - ○ flew
   - ○ off
   - ● moon
2. Which word is a noun?
   - ○ new
   - ● star
   - ○ bring
3. Which pronoun can replace the words in bold?
   **Jose and I** read about stars.
   - ○ They
   - ● We
   - ○ Them
4. Which sentence uses commas correctly?
   - ● I like to draw the sky, stars, and moon.
   - ○ We have books about rockets jets, and planes.
   - ○ Where are the books, about the Earth sun and, stars?
5. Write the sentence correctly.
   a noo rocket floo to the moone to breeng a stoan back to Earth
   A new rocket few to the moon to bring a stone back to Earth.

Ask someone to test you on the spelling words.

1.
2.
3.
4.
5.
6.
7.
8.
9.
10.

## Page 83

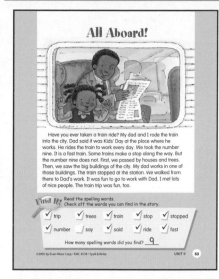

### All Aboard!

Have you ever taken a train ride? My dad and I rode the train into the city. Dad said it was Kids' Day at the place where he works. He rides the train to work every day. We took the number nine. It is a fast train. Some trains make a stop along the way. But the number nine does not. First, we passed by houses and trees. Then, we saw the big buildings of the city. My dad works in one of those buildings. The train stopped at the station. We walked from there to Dad's work. It was fun to go to work with Dad. I met lots of nice people. The train trip was fun, too.

**Find It!** Read the spelling words. Check off the words you can find in the story.

✓ trip ✓ trees ✓ train ✓ stop ✓ stopped
✓ number ☐ say ✓ said ✓ ride ✓ fast

How many spelling words did you find? **9**

## Page 85

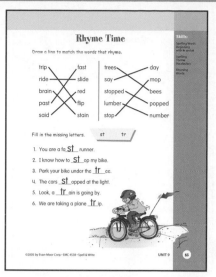

### Rhyme Time

Draw a line to match the words that rhyme.

trip — flip
ride — slide
brain — stain
past — fast
said — red

trees — bees
say — day
stopped — mop
lumber — number
stop — popped

Fill in the missing letters. **st** **tr**

1. You are a fa **st** runner.
2. I know how to **st** op my bike.
3. Park your bike under the **tr** ee.
4. The cars **st** opped at the light.
5. Look, a **tr** ain is going by.
6. We are taking a plane **tr** ip.

## Page 86

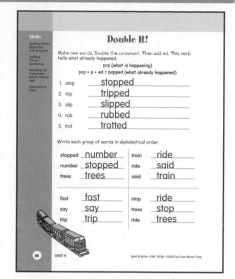

### Double It!

Make new words. Double the consonant. Then add ed. This verb tells what already happened.

pop (what is happening)
pop + p + ed = popped (what already happened)

1. stop   **stopped**
2. trip   **tripped**
3. slip   **slipped**
4. rub   **rubbed**
5. trot   **trotted**

Write each group of words in alphabetical order.

| stopped | **number** | train | **ride** |
|---|---|---|---|
| number | **stopped** | ride | **said** |
| trees | **trees** | said | **train** |

| fast | **fast** | stop | **ride** |
|---|---|---|---|
| say | **say** | trees | **stop** |
| trip | **trip** | ride | **trees** |

## Page 87

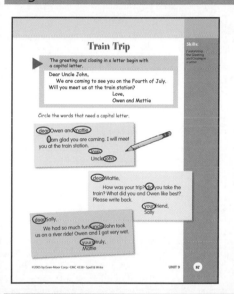

### Train Trip

The greeting and closing in a letter begin with a capital letter.

Dear Uncle John,
We are coming to see you on the Fourth of July. Will you meet us at the train station?
Love,
Owen and Mattie

Circle the words that need a capital letter.

(dear) Owen and (mattie)
(i) am glad you are coming. I will meet you at the train station.
(love)
Uncle (john)

(dear) Mattie,
How was your trip? (did) you take the train? What did you and Owen like best? Please write back.
(your) friend,
Sally

(dear) Sally,
We had so much fun (uncle) John took us on a river ride! Owen and I got very wet.
(yours) truly,
Mattie

## Page 88

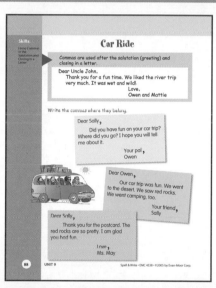

### Car Ride

Commas are used after the salutation (greeting) and closing in a letter.

Dear Uncle John,
Thank you for a fun time. We liked the river trip very much. It was wet and wild!
Love,
Owen and Mattie

Write the commas where they belong.

Dear Sally,
Did you have fun on your car trip? Where did you go? I hope you will tell me about it.
Your pal,
Owen

Dear Owen,
Our car trip was fun. We went to the desert. We saw red rocks. We went camping, too.
Your friend,
Sally

Dear Sally,
Thank you for the postcard. The red rocks are so pretty. I am glad you had fun.
Love,
Ms. May

## Page 89

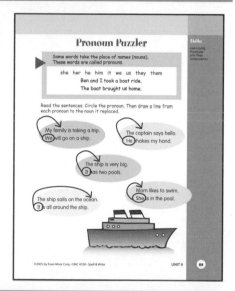

### Pronoun Puzzler

Some words take the place of names (nouns). These words are called pronouns.

she her he him it we us they them
Ben and I took a boat ride.
The boat brought us home.

Read the sentences. Circle the pronoun. Then draw a line from each pronoun to the noun it replaced.

My family is taking a trip. (We) will go on a ship.
The captain says hello. (He) shakes my hand.
The ship is very big. (It) has two pools.
Mom likes to swim. (She) is in the pool.
The ship sails on the ocean. (It) is all around the ship.

## Page 90

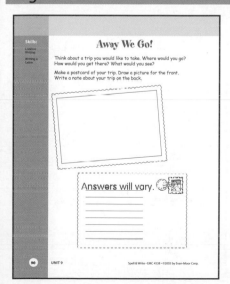

### Away We Go!

Think about a trip you would like to take. Where would you go? How would you get there? What would you see?

Make a postcard of your trip. Draw a picture for the front. Write a note about your trip on the back.

Answers will vary.

Answers will vary.

## Page 91

### Magic Train

One day, you got on a magic train. Where did you go? Write a letter to a friend about your trip. Use capital letters and commas in the greeting and closing. Use as many spelling words as you can.

| trip | trees | train | stop | stopped |
|---|---|---|---|---|
| number | say | said | ride | fast |

Answers will vary.

**✓ Check Your Story**
☐ I used a capital letter in the greeting and closing.
☐ I used a comma after the greeting and closing.
☐ I checked my spelling words.

## Page 92

**TEST YOUR SKILLS** — **All Aboard!**     **My Spelling Test**

Find the correct answer. Fill in the circle.

1. Which pronoun should replace the words in bold?
Will you ride in the front with **Hanna and me?**
○ we
○ they
● us

2. Which greeting has the correct comma?
○ Dear, June
○ Dear Mr. Brown
● Dear Tina,

3. Which closing has the correct capital letter?
● Yours truly,
○ sincerely,
○ your Friend,

4. Where do you use a greeting and a closing?
○ in a story
● in a letter
○ in a poem

5. Write the sentence correctly.
what is the number of the traine you ride home
**What is the number of the train you ride home?**

Ask someone to test you on the spelling words.

1. _____
2. _____
3. _____
4. _____
5. _____
6. _____
7. _____
8. _____
9. _____
10. _____

## Page 93

### The Birthday Party

A birthday party is so much fun! Friends come to the party. They bring presents for the birthday child. They sing the "Happy Birthday" song. Everyone plays games.

There are always good things to eat. The best part is the birthday cake. The birthday child makes a wish and blows out the candles. The wish is supposed to come true if you blow them all out. The cake is cut, and everyone has a big piece. Will there be ice cream, too? Yum!

After the party, the birthday child thanks everyone for coming and for the presents. What a great day!

**Find It!** Read the spelling words. Check off the words you can find in the story.

| ✓ cake | ✓ makes | ✓ came | ✓ games | ✓ sing |
| ✓ bring | ✓ presents | ✓ candles | ✓ party | birthday |

How many spelling words did you find? __9__

## Page 95

### Word Puzzles

Fill in the boxes with the spelling words.

bring    presents    candles    party
makes    came    games    sing

1. makes
2. sing
3. games
4. candles
5. party
6. presents
7. came
8. bring

Make word families. Write the words from the word box in the correct box below. Add more words if you can.

| rake | ring | same |
| cake | bring | games |
| make | sing | came |

bring  game
came  cake
make  sing

**Skills:**
Spelling Words with a-e and ing
Spelling Theme Vocabulary
Visual Memory and Discrimination
Word Families
Rhyming Words

## Page 96

**Skills:**
Using Context Clues to Identify Missing Words
Writing Spelling Words
Writing Complete Sentences with Correct Capitalization and Ending Punctuation

### What's Missing?

Fill in the missing spelling words.

cake    makes    came    candles    games    sing
bring    presents    party    birthday

1. Kim was six years old on her __birthday__.
2. Father made a big chocolate __cake__ for Kim's party.
3. How many guests __came__ to the party?
4. They played __games__ in the backyard.
5. Let's all __sing__ "Happy Birthday."
6. Did they bring __presents__ for the birthday girl?

Write a sentence using each of these spelling words. Begin with a capital letter. End with correct punctuation.

7. bring
___Answers will vary.___

8. candles

## Page 97

### Capitals Needed

Sentences begin with a capital letter.
> The school bus stops in front of my house.

Names of people and pets begin with a capital letter.
> Manuel has a cat named Fluffy.

Circle the words that should begin with a capital letter. The first one has been done for you.

1. (today) was (kim's) birthday.
2. (she) had a party.
3. (mike) (jill) and (tammy) came to the party.
4. (the) friends played games.
5. (mom) gave (kim) a dog.
6. (she) named her new dog (beewee).
7. (jill) and (tammy) gave her a book about (cinderella).
8. (mike) gave (kim) a big red ball.
9. (everybody) had fun at (kim's) party.

Write a sentence about you and your friends. Use capital letters.
___Answers will vary.___

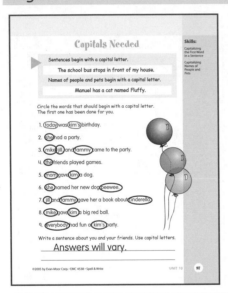

**Skills:**
Capitalizing the First Word in a Sentence
Capitalizing Names of People and Pets

## Page 98

**Skills:**
Using Correct Ending Punctuation
Writing a Statement, a Question, and an Exclamation

### Make Your Mark

Use correct punctuation marks at the ends of sentences.
✓ A telling sentence ends with a period. (.)
✓ An asking sentence ends with a question mark. (?)
✓ A sentence that shows strong feeling ends with an exclamation point. (!)

Write the correct punctuation at the end of each sentence.

1. May I have a birthday party ?
2. Who do you want to invite ?
3. Let's play games and eat in the backyard .
4. Dad will cook hot dogs on the grill .
5. Don't touch that hot grill !
6. Are you ready to eat ice cream and cake ?
7. Don't drop the birthday cake !
8. Thank you for my presents .

Write a telling sentence.
9. ___Answers will vary.___

Write an asking sentence.
10. _____

Write a sentence that shows strong feeling.
11. _____

## Page 99

### 1, 2, and 3

Use a comma (,) between words in a series.
> Carlos had a hot dog, chips, and milk for lunch.

Place commas where they are needed.

1. Mother got red, green, and yellow balloons for the party.
2. Jess asked Tom, Jay, and Kelly to his birthday party.
3. Is the party on Friday, Saturday, or Sunday?
4. Did Jess have six, seven, or eight candles on his cake?
5. Do you want chocolate, vanilla, or strawberry ice cream with your cake?
6. I decorated the present with blue ribbon, a white bow, and a gold star.
7. Jess got a bike, a football, and a game for his birthday.

Write a sentence about a birthday party that lists three things in a series.
___Answers will vary.___

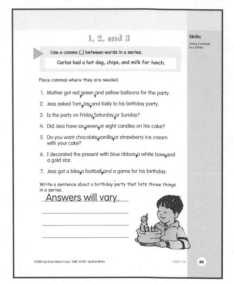

**Skills:**
Using Commas in a Series

## Page 100

**Skills:**
Writing Complete Sentences

### Birthday Questionnaire

Your parents are planning a birthday party for you. Here are some questions they would like you to answer. Write your answers in complete sentences.

1. Where do you want to have your birthday party?
___Answers will vary.___

2. Who do you want to invite to your party?
_____

3. What do you want to eat at your party?
_____

4. What games do you want to play at your party?
_____

5. How many candles should be on your birthday cake?
_____

6. What presents would you like for your birthday?
_____

## Page 101

### A Funny Birthday Party

Write a story about a birthday party for a pet dog named Sam. Use as many spelling words as you can.

cake    makes    came    games    sing
bring    presents    candles    party    birthday

___Answers will vary.___

_____

**Check Your Story**
○ I wrote complete sentences.
○ I used capital letters where they were needed.
○ I used correct punctuation marks.

**Skills:**
Writing a Creative Story
Using Spelling Words in a Composition
Using Correct Capitalization and Punctuation

## Page 102

**TEST YOUR SKILLS — The Birthday Party**

**My Spelling Test**
Ask someone to test you on the spelling words.

Find the correct answer. Fill in the circle.

1. Which punctuation mark goes at the end of the sentence?
   How many children came to the birthday party___
   ○ period (.)
   ● question mark (?)
   ○ exclamation point (!)

2. Which punctuation mark goes at the end of the sentence?
   That was the best chocolate cake I've ever had___
   ○ period (.)
   ○ question mark (?)
   ● exclamation mark (!)

3. Which group of words should begin with a capital letter?
   ○ a birthday present.
   ● they played games at the party.
   ○ eating birthday cake.

4. Where should the commas go in this sentence?
   Jill Mike and Tammy came to the party.
   ● Jill, Mike, and Tammy
   ○ Jill, Mike, and, Tammy
   ○ Jill, Mike and Tammy

5. Write the sentence correctly.
   did sam bring a presunt to my birthda partee
   ___Did Sam bring a present to my birthday party?___

1. _____
2. _____
3. _____
4. _____
5. _____
6. _____
7. _____
8. _____
9. _____
10. _____

**142**

Spell & Write • EMC 4538 • © Evan-Moor Corp.

## Page 103

**Bunny Puppets**

We had fun in art class today. Mrs. Green showed us how to make something new. We made bunny puppets! Here's how to make the puppet. First, paint a stick. Then cut two paper circles. One circle is the head, and one is the body. You could use any color paper you wish. My bunny is brown. Glue the circles to the stick. Then draw two round eyes. Draw a triangle nose. Then make two long ears. Glue them onto the bunny. Put a ball of cotton on the back for a tail. Now, give your bunny a name. I named my bunny Floppy. I can make Floppy hop around.

**Find It!** Read the spelling words. Check off the words you can find in the story.

☑ could ☐ would ☑ found ☑ round ☑ around
☑ something ☑ brown ☑ green ☑ draw ☑ paint

How many spelling words did you find? __8__

## Page 105

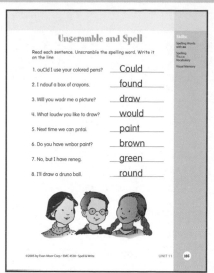

**Unscramble and Spell**

Read each sentence. Unscramble the spelling word. Write it on the line.

1. ouCld I use your colored pens? __Could__
2. I ndouf a box of crayons. __found__
3. Will you wadr me a picture? __draw__
4. What loudw you like to draw? __would__
5. Next time we can pntai. __paint__
6. Do you have wnbor paint? __brown__
7. No, but I have reneg. __green__
8. I'll draw a druno ball. __round__

## Page 106

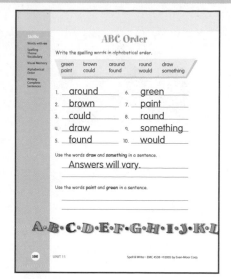

**ABC Order**

Write the spelling words in alphabetical order.

| green | brown | around | round | draw |
| paint | could | found | would | something |

1. __around__   6. __green__
2. __brown__   7. __paint__
3. __could__   8. __round__
4. __draw__   9. __something__
5. __found__   10. __would__

Use the words **draw** and **something** in a sentence.
__Answers will vary.__

Use the words **paint** and **green** in a sentence.

A·B·C·D·E·F·G·H·I·J·K·L

## Page 107

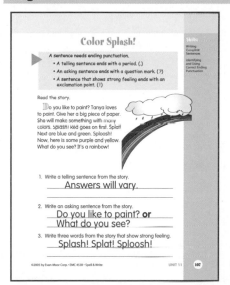

**Color Splash!**

▸ A sentence needs ending punctuation.
• A telling sentence ends with a period. (.)
• An asking sentence ends with a question mark. (?)
• A sentence that shows strong feeling ends with an exclamation point. (!)

Read the story.

Do you like to paint? Tanya loves to paint. Give her a big piece of paper. She will make something with many colors. Splash! Red goes on first. Splat! Next are blue and green. Sploosh! Now, here is some purple and yellow. What do you see? It's a rainbow!

1. Write a telling sentence from the story.
__Answers will vary.__

2. Write an asking sentence from the story.
__Do you like to paint?__ **or** __What do you see?__

3. Write three words from the story that show strong feeling.
__Splash! Splat! Sploosh!__

## Page 108

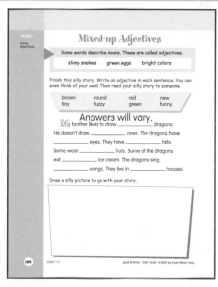

**Mixed-up Adjectives**

Some words describe nouns. These are called adjectives.

slimy snakes    green eggs    bright colors

Finish this silly story. Write an adjective in each sentence. You can even think of your own! Then read your silly story to someone.

| brown | round | red | new |
| tiny | fuzzy | green | funny |

__Answers will vary.__

My brother likes to draw _____ dragons.
He doesn't draw _____ ones. The dragons have _____ eyes. They have _____ tails.
Some wear _____ hats. Some of the dragons eat _____ ice cream. The dragons sing _____ songs. They live in _____ houses.

Draw a silly picture to go with your story.

## Page 109

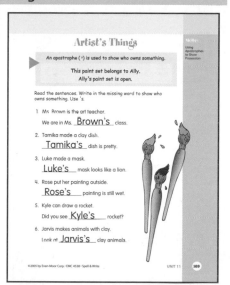

**Artist's Things**

▸ An apostrophe (') is used to show who owns something.

This paint set belongs to Ally.
Ally's paint set is open.

Read the sentences. Write in the missing word to show who owns something. Use 's.

1. Ms. Brown is the art teacher.
We are in Ms. __Brown's__ class.

2. Tamika made a clay dish.
__Tamika's__ dish is pretty.

3. Luke made a mask.
__Luke's__ mask looks like a lion.

4. Rose put her painting outside.
__Rose's__ painting is still wet.

5. Kyle can draw a rocket.
Did you see __Kyle's__ rocket?

6. Jarvis makes animals with clay.
Look at __Jarvis's__ clay animals.

## Page 110

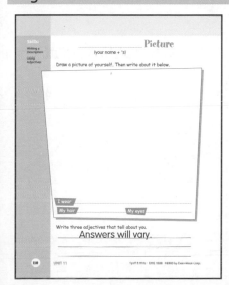

**Picture**
(your name + 's)

Draw a picture of yourself. Then write about it below.

I wear
My hair          My eyes

Write three adjectives that tell about you.
__Answers will vary.__

## Page 111

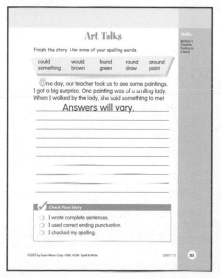

**Art Talks**

Finish the story. Use some of your spelling words.

| could | would | found | round | around |
| something | brown | green | draw | paint |

One day, our teacher took us to see some paintings. I got a big surprise. One painting was of a smiling lady. When I walked by the lady, she said something to me!

__Answers will vary.__

✓ **Check Your Story**
○ I wrote complete sentences.
○ I used correct ending punctuation.
○ I checked my spelling.

## Page 112

**TEST YOUR SKILLS** — Bunny Puppets | My Spelling Test

Find the correct answer. Fill in the circle.

1. Which sentence has the correct ending?
○ I like to paint?
○ How did you draw that.
● Did you use a red crayon?

2. Which sentence has the correct ending punctuation?
● Don't spill the paint!
○ Where are the brushes.
○ I like your picture?

3. Which word is an adjective?
○ picture
● green
○ draw

4. Which word describes the underlined word?
I made a round dish in art class.
○ class
○ made
● round

5. Write the sentence correctly.
may I pante grean flowers around Amys drawing
__May I paint green flowers around Amy's drawing?__

Ask someone to test you on the spelling words.
1.
2.
3.
4.
5.
6.
7.
8.
9.
10.

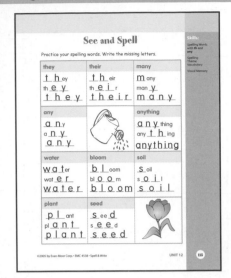

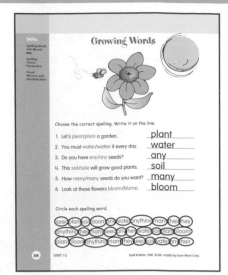

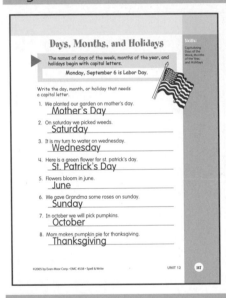

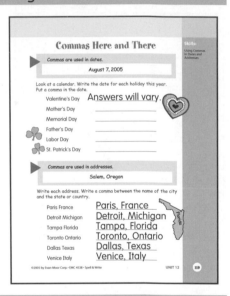

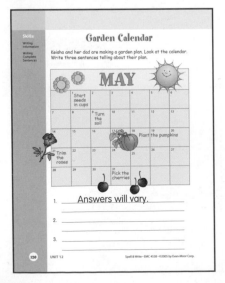

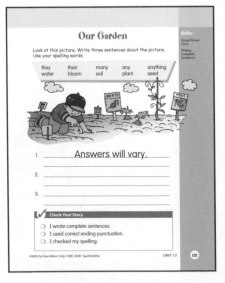

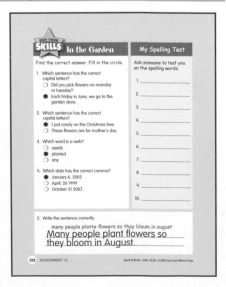